IUNDS A

Based on a plan by A.B.Whittingham

SAINT EDMUND — KING AND MARTYR

SAINT EDMUND — KING AND MARTYR

by

BRYAN HOUGHTON

TERENCE DALTON LIMITED
LAVENHAM . SUFFOLK
1970

Published by
TERENCE DALTON LIMITED
S B N 900963 18 2

Photo Engravings by
STAR ILLUSTRATION WORKS LIMITED

Printed in Great Britain at
THE LAVENHAM PRESS LIMITED
LAVENHAM SUFFOLK

Contents

Illustrations

To
Monsieur Edmond Bordier
without whose constant nagging this
Essay would never have been written.

Acknowledgements

The Author and the Publishers would like to express their appreciation for the help and co-operation they have received in searching for and obtaining illustrations.

We are very grateful to Mr. L. Payne of the Bury St Edmunds Borough Council. He was instrumental in bringing Author and Publisher together and has co-operated with help and advice from that time onwards. We would also like to thank the College Gateway Bookshop in Ipswich whose thoughtfulness and kindness in anticipating our needs deserve recognition.

In the first section of pictures we are grateful for the help received from The British Museum and The National Gallery. Also to the Pierpont Morgan Library, New York for reproductions from their manuscript, M 736. This was the "Miracula sancti Eadmundi, regis et martyris; Abbon of Fleury, Passio sancti Eadmundi; Officium sancti Eadmundi". It consists of the Miracles of St Edmund, king and martyr, in two books; preceded by copies of documents of Henry I, Abbot Anselm and Prior Talebot of the Abbey of Bury St Edmunds and followed by the Passion of St Edmund by Abbon of Fleury (945-1004) with the dedication to Archbishop Dunstan (925-988) and the Office for the feast of St Edmund. The manuscript is on vellum, was written in Latin and illuminated in the Abbey of Bury St Edmunds in the middle of the twelfth century.

In this first and in the second section we are grateful for the skill and help of three local photographers—Richard Burn of Sudbury, Studio Five of Thetford and Walter Blythin of Clacton on Sea.

Also in the second or middle section we would like to thank Mr. E. E. Swain of Hunstanton who not only took photographs but also kindly researched the exact locations. M. B.Saltel of 6 Rue des Chalets, Toulouse provided the excellent pictures from France.

In the last section we are extremely grateful to Mr. W. Appel, Editor of the Bury Free Press and his staff whose help and co-operation made it possible to include a whole section on the Bury St Edmunds Abbey.

Finally our thanks to the Ministry of Public Buildings and Works for permission to use the site plan of the Abbey. This was ably drawn for the Ministry by Mr. A. B. Whittingham of Norwich, one of the best known authorities on the Abbey to-day. It is to Mr. Whittingham we express thanks not only for allowing us to use his plan but also for kindly advising us on captions relating to the Abbey.

Preface

In 1954 I was appointed to St Edmund's Parish at Bury St Edmunds. All I knew about St Edmund was that he had been a King of East Anglia in the ninth century; that he had been killed by the Danes; that Arundel possessed his spurious relics. I was sufficiently occupied by my living parishioners not to bother about the dead ones; St Edmund received scant attention.

In 1959 some wretched Frenchman started badgering me about St Edmund. He took it for granted that, as Parish Priest of Bury St Edmunds, I was a mine of information on my patron. At first, of course, I paid not the slightest attention. But human nature is frail and, once we have surrendered to temptation, we slip ineluctably down the slope to perdition. A tart acknowledgement was enough for M. Edmond Bordier, for such was his name, to redouble his activities. I soon found myself immersed in Edmundiana.

By 1966 I knew quite a lot about him. I had acquired a library, probably unique, on St Edmund. It included an irreplaceable manuscript by the late J. R. Thompson, author of "The Records of St Edmund" (1890), given to me by Mr. Geoffrey Houghton-Brown. Mrs Alan Rowe had given me a photostat of a manuscript at Douai. I had others from Toulouse, Lucca and elsewhere. I was preparing to burden the world with a learned treatise, complete with footnotes, appendices, tables and indeces.

A large and busy parish is not ideally suited, however, for producing such a work. It would have to be done over several years during my holidays. To this end, St Edmund's library was annually installed in the back of my car. Unfortunately, in 1966, a friend had lent me an enormous left-hand-drive Jaguar. The back seat was big enough for St Edmund all right. I had been down to Lucca and was returning to Toulouse when the car was stolen. Curiously enough, the thieves were not in the least interested in St Edmund; they merely wanted a large and fast limousine to help in a bank robbery. My Edmundiana was thrown out of the back and scattered wide over the Alps. St Edmund, obviously, did not want a learned treatise. The present study is what he will get instead.

The general literature on St Edmund is fortunately of easy access and of very high quality. Apart from the vast mine of documents in the Monasticon (ed. 1846), it can be summed up as follows.

In 1890, J. R. Thompson published his Records of St. Edmund. This is a charming and readable little book. It is surprising that it has not been brought up-to-date and reprinted.

In 1893, Prior Mackinlay produced his Life of St Edmund. It is still the best known biography. It is full of information and well worth reading but is curiously uncritical.

In 1895, Dr Montague James published his History of the Abbey of Bury St Edmunds. It is rather learned but is an example of what such a work should be. James has an endearing prejudice; his beloved monks at Bury could do no wrong!

In 1896, Arnold edited the Memorials of St Edmund's Abbey in the Rolls Series. This again is an exemplary work. It contains all the sources for the first half of the following study: Abbo's account of the martyrdom; Geoffrey of Wells' account of St Edmund's childhood; Archdeacon Hermann's History, and the rest.

In 1901, Sir Ernest Clarke enlarged on a letter he had written to The Times and published it as a booklet called "The Bones of St Edmund". It contains the principal arguments against the authenticity of the Toulouse relics. It will consequently have to receive, in the present study, more attention than is its due.

In 1907, Lord Francis Hervey edited his beautiful book, the Corolla Sancti Edmundi. It contains the text with translations of Abbo and Geoffrey of Wells, along with extracts from relevant chronicles. It also prints Denis Piramus' beautiful Normano-French poem and Lydgate's verse. It would be churlish to criticise the editing or translations; although neither are faultless. Already in 1886 Lord Francis had published a pamphlet against the authenticity of the Toulouse relics. He is always eminently readable but was over-endowed with imagination. He felt unable to let his sources speak for themselves.

After Lord Francis, little was written about St Edmund, except in passing, until M. Edmond Bordier published his admirable "Vivant Saint Edmond" (Editions du Cèdre, Paris, 1961), on which the present study depends for most, but not all, of its information concerning the Toulouse evidence.

In 1966, Antonia Gransden edited the Bury Chronicle, an important event in itself although, because of its dates, it has little bearing on the present study.

Those are the principal sources of this little book. Because of the enormous period of time it covers, it has not been easy to write. It is to be hoped that it will be easier to read.

CHAPTER ONE

Charlemagne, Edmund, Alfred

In 929 King Athelstan, the grandson of Alfred the Great, made a tour of the shrines of his kingdom. In due course he arrived at Bury St Edmunds. It was of particular interest to him. His grandfather had known Edmund personally and had held him in high esteem. In those days, of course, Alfred was no more than the brother of the King of Wessex, whereas Edmund had been the anointed King of East Anglia for over ten years. If no more than a decade older, Edmund was vastly his senior in experience. Should Alfred ever succeed his brother on the throne of Wessex, he would take King Edmund as his model.

There is nothing like sharing camp life and fighting side by side to reveal a man's character. Alfred and Edmund had fought together against the Danes at the siege of Nottingham in 868. It was not a very glorious campaign but Athelstan, who was only six when his grandfather died, thought he remembered him exonerating Edmund from blame. After the Danes had retired to York, Alfred had spent a few particularly happy days at Crowland Abbey in Edmund's company. It was Edmund who had suggested to Burrhed, King of Mercia, that he should make some gesture of gratitude to God for the recovery of his capital. Burrhed had complied by granting the island of Crowland to the Abbey. Alfred's and Edmund's signatures are side by side as witnesses to the gift. The two princes had gone to Crowland to implement the Charter. That was in August, 868. It was the last time Alfred and Edmund met. Fifteen months later, on November 20th, 869, Edmund had been butchered.

Now, it is a very different matter to read about the Martyrs of Ancient Rome, as Alfred did at Mass, and to have your host of the previous year martyred in your native land. Athelstan was well aware of the shock it had given his grandfather. Although conversion is a complicated thing and has a multitude of causes, the martyrdom of Edmund probably played a greater part than the admonitions of his bishops, the exhortations of his dear cousin, St Neot, or even his own misfortunes, to determine his grandfather to be a truly Christian king.

In fact, it was Alfred who had canonised Edmund. He had minted coins with himself "Ælfred Rex" on the one side and "Sc Eadmund

Rex'' on the other. On some he had even left his own name out; it was the currency of Saint Edmund the King. The fact that the pagans had butchered him had not deprived him of his kingdom but had added a more glorious title. It was all rather typical of grandfather; he was not the sort of man you could push about easily.

What rather edified Athelstan was that the Danes themselves had imitated these coins well before 890. They were still in use at the time of his visit to Bury in 929. It was a sort of act of reparation, that the murderers should recognise the sanctity of the murdered. The two races that now dominated England, Danes and Anglo-Saxons, had some chance of uniting, with a common religion and a common patron.

All this and a host of telling details, unknown to us, were present in the King's mind upon his visit to Bury. He hoped to learn much more. He did. The Abbot of the secular canons, who then kept the shrine of the saint, was able to produce an eye-witness to Edmund's martyrdom. He was about 75. He had been Edmund's armour bearer on the fatal day, sixty years before. He had been a mere lad in his early teens.

Over the years, of course, his story had become highly polished. He had got all the gestures right. A friendly canon had helped him to lard it with appropriate piety and decorate it with elegant quotations. It was really very moving. It was recited to all distinguished guests and delivered at important pilgrimages.

How long Athelstan stayed in Bury is unknown, but if he was there for a few days he is unlikely to have heard the story only once. Such stories were the popular music of those distant days: the record was played and played again until it could be hummed by heart.

Among Athelstan's clerks was a young man aged about 20, sensitive, immensely intelligent, pious: St Dunstan, the future Archbishop of Canterbury. He was deeply impressed. He took a mental record of the story in order to play it over to himself. For the rest of his long life, he would switch on ''the Passion of Edmund, King and Martyr'' at the slightest provocation. One of his numerous auditors was Abbo of Fleury, who committed it to writing in about the year 985. Abbo was so confident of his accuracy that he dedicated his account to Dunstan himself.

This is the primary source for the martyrdom of St Edmund. It could scarcely be better: the evidence of an eye-witness transmitted by a great Archbishop, himself a saint. As has been said, the account was larded with piety and decorated with quotations, in part doubtless by the old veteran himself, in part by Dunstan, and yet again by Abbo, but the underlying story remains unimpeachable.

Indeed, in a way, it is the truth of the story which makes it unsatisfactory. It deals merely with the events of the martyrdom at which the armour-bearer was present. It does not mention the campaign which preceded it, presumably because he did not fight in it; no event in the King's reign is recorded, presumably because he was too young and knew of none. Apart from the fatal day the work contains little more than the general description of a charming man and a Christian king.

It does, however, tell us who St Edmund was in the vague sort of way in which a young and humble subject was likely to know it. "Edmund, apparently, was the scion of a noble house among the Old Saxons, but being descended from the erstwhile kings (of East Anglia), he was not so much elected by right of succession as forced to sway the sceptre by the people of those provinces." (NOTE: Abbo's latin reads, ". . . . ex antiquorum saxonum nobili prosapia oriundus . . . . qui atavis regibus editus . . . . omnium comprovincialium unanimi favore non tantum eligitur ex generis succesione quantum rapitur, ut eis praeesset sceptrigera potestate."). It is very much as though, 900 years later, in writing about the accession of George I, one were to say: a scion of the house of Hanover, he was descended from the Stuarts, but succeeded rather by Act of Parliament than by mere hereditary right.

In his Corolla Sancti Edmundi, Lord Francis Hervey has tried, with as much learning as ingenuity, to make out that Edmund was the nephew of one Athelstan of Kent and consequently related to the House of Wessex. But Abbo's text simply will not bear such an interpretation. "Atavis regibus editus", descended from ancient kings, cannot refer to the ruling House of Wessex since it means "descended from erstwhile kings". This is clear because it is a quotation from Horace which the poet addresses to Micaenas. Now Micaenas was descended from the erstwhile kings of Aretium; he was in no way connected with the Emperor Augustus. In the same way, Edmund was descended from the erstwhile kings of East Anglia and was in no way connected with King Athelstan whom the armour-bearer was addressing.

So Edmund came from Old Saxony, Continental Saxony, from somewhere between the valleys of the Ems and the Elbe, but was nonetheless a descendant of the House of Uffa, which had reigned in East Anglia for over 250 years, from the middle of the sixth century to 794 when King Ethelbert was murdered by Offa of Mercia.

On the face of it this is by no means unlikely. The eighth century had witnessed an event which changed the whole history of Europe: Charlemagne's conquest of Saxony, completed in 775. From then onwards the Christian, Mediterranean culture had reached the continental shores of the North Sea and Baltic; modern Germany had been created. Charlemagne forced Christianity on the Saxons at the point of the sword, but he was not so foolish as to imagine that a sword takes root. The Gospel had to be preached and lived in the conquered territories. The obvious way to evangelise the Old Saxons was through the already Christianised Anglo-Saxons. Such was his deliberate policy and the fact that his Secretary of State for the Department of Education and Science was Alcuin was due as much to his being a Northumbrian as to his personal merit.

It is precisely at this point, in 794, that Offa of Mercia assassinated King Ethelbert of East Anglia and attempted to annex the kingdom. The following fifty years saw chaos in East Anglia. It was an unhealthy time for the princelets of the House of Uffa. If some doubtless preserved a shadowy show of independence in the marshlands, some, more exposed, sought refuge at the court of the great emperor. Charlemagne would have received them with open arms. One thing was certain about the Saxons: they were colossal snobs. To have a Christian member of the House of Uffa, descended in direct line from their own pagan god, Woden, was just the man to make kinglet of some remote part of Saxony.

None of this of course can be proven. What can and must be said, however, is that Abbo's statement rings perfectly possible of the time about which he was writing—say A.D.800, although it must have seemed very strange already at the time when in fact he wrote, in 985.

CHAPTER TWO

From Cradle to Crown

To have a formal account of St Edmund's background and youth, one has to wait nearly 200 years, until 1150. We are now 300 years after the event. What possible historical value can such evidence have? What is the value of what I know by common consent about the birth and childhood of Queen Anne? It is by no means valueless, but, unlike the evidence of an eye-witness, preserved in Abbo, it can legitimately be contradicted if it fails to fit the known facts and can scarcely be taken for certain unless corroborated from other sources.

The author of the work on St Edmund's youth was one Geoffrey of Wells. He was probably a native of Wells-next-the-Sea in Norfolk and certainly an Augustinian Canon of Thetford, also in Norfolk. His evidence consequently has the enormous advantage of being in part unrelated to the tradition of Bury, although he was *persona grata* at the Abbey and a personal friend of Abbot Ording (A.D. 1148-56).

This is the outline of Geoffrey's story.

The king of East Anglia before Edmund was called Offa. He had no heir. He decided to go on a pilgrimage to the Holy Land to pray that God might grant him one. "So he made arrangements to pass through the kingdom of Saxony, where the king was his relative, whose advice would be most useful on undertaking so arduous a journey". Offa was received royally at the Saxon court and the local king ordered his two sons to wait on him. The younger of these was Edmund. Offa was quite overcome at meeting a young man so considerate and well-mannered ("studiosum et elegantem"); and was as "delighted by his conversation as flattered by his attention".

As far as Offa was concerned, his prayer had been answered at the start of his pilgrimage. Edmund should be his heir. This was solemnly proclaimed in front of the Saxon court. A ring was placed on Edmund's finger to signify the adoption, with the promise of the royal signet when Offa died. Edmund's father is said to have accepted the arrangement with hearty good humour: "Well I'm blowed! So that's how you get rid of me! you take this king of East Anglia for your father. It's up to him now to make you an allowance and you had better sponge on him as your father. Why should I educate another man's boy?" Everybody laughed and Offa set off to the Holy Land light of heart. Incidentally Geoffrey mentions that he did not travel light; "he left with a great deal of baggage".

Offa duly arrived at Jerusalem and poured out his soul in prayer and praise, but he never returned home. He died in the Straits known as "St George's Arm". Before his death he reminded his companions of his adoption of Edmund and gave them the royal signet-ring to hand over to him.

Offa's companions made haste to Saxony, presented Edmund with the ring and demanded his return with them to England. The Saxon king demurred until he remembered the prophecy of a holy widow whom he had met during one of his visits to Rome. It is an impossible story and one wonders if Geoffrey has got it quite right. He seems to have realised that it was unconvincing and so reinforces it: "the King remembered these strange events and told them exactly as they had been written down"—yes, yes! Anyway the king gave in and Edmund sailed for England.

The party landed, not, as one might have expected somewhere near Orford or Caister, but right round the Norfolk coast at Maidensbure by Hunstanton, where in later years Edmund built a royal residence. It is not all that far from Sandringham where there is still a royal residence, so little do things change in spite of a thousand years and a thousand revolutions.

Edmund does not appear to have stayed long in the neighbourhood of the Wash since it was the same men, the companions of the late Offa, who brought him to Attleborough. Here things went wrong. "The instruments of the devil" made him wait a whole year before there was any question of proclaiming him king. Edmund passed the time in learning the Psalter by heart.

Incidentally, this was not an uncommon practice. It must be remembered that in a society largely illiterate from necessity, through lack of paper, the first object of education was to train the memory. How could this better be done than by means of the Psalter? Apart from the memory as such, on the practical side it would give the student a wide vocabulary, on the artistic an appreciation of sublime poetry, on the moral a sense of humility, and finally on the religious a realisation of the transcendence of God. Edmund consequently was by no means an uneducated barbarian.

At the end of a year, however, the time seemed ripe to proclaim

Edmund king. Geoffrey gives two reasons: firstly, the coasts of Norfolk were already being de-populated by pirates from across the sea; secondly, the neighbouring kings of Mercia and Wessex wished to annex the provinces of East Anglia. This last remark has some historic importance. It shows that Geoffrey had never come across any indication that Edmund was precisely a puppet of Wessex, and, indeed, related to that kingdom's royal house. As far as the evidence in front of him went, the exact opposite was the truth.

A moot of the provinces was called and the bishop, Humbert, supported by the principal nobles proposed the election of Edmund to the throne. A king had become an urgent necessity to them all. Edmund, a close relative of the late king who had, moreover, designated him as heir, was the obvious candidate. Edmund was duly acclaimed. He was fetched from Attleborough and hurried off to the royal town of Bures on the "fast flowing Stour" where he was anointed and crowned on Christmas Day, 855. Incidentally the traditional spot of the coronation is a hill above Bures with one of the most beautiful views in Suffolk. It is also marked by a singularly lovely chapel, consecrated in 1218 by Stephen Langton, Archbishop of Canterbury, to which some of the tombs of the De Vere's, Earls of Oxford, were transferred from Earls Colne in Essex.

Having got his hero "to the apex of kingly power" Geoffrey practically leaves him there. He gives no detail of Edmund's 14 years of reign. Like Abbo, he falls back on generalities, doubtless perfectly true: "he was as firm of purpose as merciful in action". But what were his policies and what he accomplished remain unknown.

Geoffrey ends his little treatise with the story as to why the Danes invaded East Anglia. The infamous Danish pirate, Lodebrok, begat three execrable sons, to wit Hingwar, Ubba and Bern. Geoffrey gives Ubba a particularly bad write-up as a practitioner of black magic. It is of course true that ritual cannibalism was not unknown to the Danes. Anyway, their father upbraided them for their lack of success in life: "why, look at that young fellow Edmund! Only a few years ago he arrived from Saxony and landed in England with a handful of followers; now he is master of East Anglia. Have you ever done the like? You degenerate puppies!" Out of filial respect and to show themselves worthy sons of such a father they invaded East Anglia, conquered the country and murdered the king. It is as simple as that.

Before attempting a critical appreciation of Geoffrey of Wells it is worth while examining the final form of the legend in Bury St Edmunds.

This dates from the time of Abbot Curteys, between 1429 and 1446. Its historical value is not considerable.

The parents of St Edmund are given names; Alkmund and Siware. They seem unlikely. Why should they have been unknown to Geoffrey of Wells? Siware was certainly the name of the mother of St. Botolph, whose arm was among the relics of Bury. There may have been some mis-filing among the Bury records. Edmund is given a date of birth: 841. This is possible but unlikely; it makes him very young to have been elected king expressly to repulse the Danish pirates. He is said to have been born in Saxony at "Norhemberges". Undue scorn has been poured upon this assertion; the incredible blunder of placing Nüremberg in Saxony! But suppose it is a mis-copy for North Hamburg, that is the Saxon territory north of the Elbe, the Carolingian area known as Transalbingia, the modern Holstein? It would surely be among the areas where Charlemagne would have most welcomed a Christian prince of the House of Uffa.

Where the Bury tradition becomes highly imaginative is in the reasons it gives for the great Danish invasion. After quoting Geoffrey concerning Lodebrok jeering at his execrable sons, but only two of them—Hingwar and Ubba—it proceeds to relate how Lodebrok went out duck-shooting in a dinghy and got carried across the North Sea by a storm to Reedham in Norfolk. Edmund received him so graciously that he became a court favourite. Edmund's chief huntsman, Bern, grew jealous and murdered Lodebrok. The crime was revealed and the criminal unmasked by Lodebrok's greyhound. Sentence was passed on Bern: he was embarked oarless in his victim's dinghy which was promptly blown back across the North Sea and was met by Hingwar and Ubba. Bern of course explained how it was Edmund, not he, who had murdered Lodebrok. The execrable sons invaded East Anglia to avenge the murder of their father.

Incidentally, whoever was the father of Hingwar, Ubba and Bern or Wern (alias Alfdene), he was unlikely to be the great pirate Ragnar Lodebrok who sacked Paris in 845, because the dates will scarcely fit. But, absurd as this story may be, it illustrates two facts: the Danes had an excellent intelligence system in England and treason among the Anglo-Saxons was by no means unknown.

Let us now attempt to give an historical appreciation of Geoffrey of Wells. Was the immediate predecessor of St Edmund on the throne of East Anglia called Offa? Did he go to the Holy Land and die before his return? Is Edmund likely to have landed at Hunstanton, and the like? What were the causes of the Danish invasion?

King Offa appears to present a real difficulty. Both from history and from coinage the king of East Anglia immediately before Edmund was Athelstan of Kent, of the House of Wessex, presumably the son of King Egbert and consequently uncle of Alfred the Great. How this had come about was reasonably simple. As has already been seen, in 794, Offa, King of Mercia, murdered the last independent king of East Anglia of the House of Uffa. East Anglia became a dependency of Mercia until Egbert of Wessex overthrew the predominance of Mercia in about 825. The kingdom then passed into the dependency of Wessex.

But what real power did these foreign kings wield? It must be remembered that in those days Norfolk and Suffolk formed a peninsula attached to the mainland by the narrow chalk escarpment where the A45 runs through Newmarket. To the south it was cut off from Essex by "the fast flowing Stour", with impenetrable forest in its upper regions and unpassable marshes at its mouth. On the west Ely was an island and the fens of the undrained Wash stretched right up to Cambridge. Doubtless an overking of Mercia or Wessex could control the approaches easily enough, the road at Newmarket and the passage of the Stour at Bures, but he was most unlikely to have any real control of Norfolk at all. Indeed, there is no indication that any of these overlords ever set foot on East Anglian soil. Even Athelstan of Kent, the predecessor of Edmund, disappears from history in 851. The kings of Wessex do not seem to have nominated a successor. Their position might compare with those kings of England who styled themselves kings of France right up to the reign of George III, by which time they had ceased to have any pretention to rule the country for some 400 years. The statement of William of Malmesbury is undoubtedly correct: "After King Ethelbert few reigned in East Anglia with any real authority up to the time of St Edmund owing to the violence of the Mercians".

In his Corolla Sancti Edmundi, Lord Francis Hervey has collected the evidence of coinage. It is desperately fragmentary. Of the kings of Mercia, those who could best claim overlordship of East Anglia, Offa, the murderer of Ethelbert, and his immediate successors Egfrith and Cenulph, do not appear to have minted in the province; whereas those who could not claim overlordship, Beornwolf, Berhtulf and Burrhed, did. Of the kings and princes of the House of Wessex, Athelstan I of Kent certainly minted, but so did King Ethelred, even during the life time of Edmund himself! As for the Danes, Athelstan II Guthrum minted all right, but his known successors Eric and

Athelstan III did not! The slenderness of this evidence must also be remembered. The catalogue of J. J. North (English Hammered Coinage, Vol. 1) gives the following specimens: Beonna (c.758) 1; Ethelbert (murdered 794) 1; Edwald (c.796) 3; Athelstan I (c.845) 16; Æthelweard (c.850) 7; St Edmund 7. Under such circumstances it is not surprising that no coin has been found of Geoffrey's King Offa.

Before leaving the coinage a small point may be cleared up. Lord Francis Hervey mentions some coins of a King Aldulf who died in 713. In fact these coins are more likely to belong to Alfdene Rx. North places them around 900. But Alfdene was the third brother of Hingwar and Ubba, whom Geoffrey calls Bern (see R. H. Hodgkin, "History of the Anglo-Saxons," Oxford, 1935). The coin must have been minted between 869, the death of St Edmund, and 878 when Athelstan II started to mint. This would imply that Alfdene was left in East Anglia while his coinless brothers turned their attention to Wessex.

Geoffrey's story becomes particularly cogent from the fact that Edmund is made to land at Hunstanton and has to wait a whole year for his election. Hunstanton is about as remote as possible from the Devil's Dyke at Newmarket and Bures on the Stour, where the Wessex overlord was likely to be strongest. Attleborough was, perhaps, as far south as safety allowed him to live. It enters the picture perfectly. While Edmund was learning the Psalter, Bishop Humbert and the notables were busy negotiating with the emissaries of Wessex and their Suffolk dependents. When agreement was reached it was precisely at Bures that Edmund was crowned.

Geoffrey's general reliability receives support from two other circumstances to which, perhaps, insufficient attention has been paid. He makes his King Offa die in the river or strait called the Arm of St George. At the time when he wrote (c. 1150) this was not the St George's Channel we now know but the Dardanelles. Since he may have had no means of knowing where it was it illustrates the accuracy of his sources.

Stranger, perhaps, is a very roundabout piece of evidence. Hermann the Archdeacon, writing about the verification of St Edmund's body by Bishop Ailwin in 1032, mentions in passing how the Bishop, now blind, was able to feel that the incorrupt body had not been tampered with because the relic of the True Cross on St Edmund's breast was there as he had left it. Now, this relic of the True Cross cannot have got round St Edmund's neck after death. It must already have been on him on the fatal day of November 20th 869. Doubtless he clutched it as he met his martyrdom.

Yes, but relics of the True Cross were not easily come by in the ninth century. There were only four sources: the Patriarch of Jerusalem, the Emperor at Constantinople, the Pope of Rome and the Emperor of the West. It so happens that the earliest record of a relic of the True Cross coming to England is the fragment given to St. Neot by Pope Marinus I in 884*. This St Neot gave to Alfred the Great who passed it on to Glastonbury. It is highly probable that it is the fragment preserved to this day at Downside Abbey. How did St Edmund get an earlier relic? None can say, but the most probable explanation is that Offa got it in Jerusalem. Along with the regal signet-ring Edmund received the relic. This relic of the Cross plays its tiny part in the story of St Edmund.

To sum up, Geoffrey of Wells cannot be dismissed as a writer of legend. Where his story can be verified it seems at least probable. It amounts to this: after the assassination of King Ethelbert, princes of the House of Uffa continued to reign in Norfolk, although Suffolk was largely controlled at first by the kings of Mercia and later by the kings of Wessex. Some members of the old royal family moved to the Continent and were entrusted with the administration of the extreme northern area of Old Saxony. Upon the imminent extinction of the English branch, its last representative, one Offa, adopted a young cousin of the Saxon branch. This was Edmund. Edmund inherited Offa's principality without difficulty. Circumstances, notably the de-population of the coast owing to Danish piracy with which the Wessex overlords were unable to cope, led to the restoration of an independent East Anglian monarchy in his person. He was crowned at Bures on Christmas Day, 855. All this must stand.

The real causes of the Danish invasion, as opposed to mere piracy, were as mysterious to Geoffrey as they still are to us: hence the fiction of Lodebrok. This, however, should be said. Charlemagne's conquest of Saxony had completely upset the balance of power in northern Europe. Pagan Scandinavia, which had spread right across the north of the Continent, had almost become reduced to the Baltic States. Inevitably England became a frontier. Were these islands to be a

*NOTE. In his admirable monograph on St Neot, Mr Houghton-Brown refers to the Pope as Martin II, according to the common practice in the Middle Ages.

northern outpost of Mediterranean Europe or a western outpost of Scandinavia? The problem has never quite been solved. Even today, ought we to join the Common Market or remain in our predominantly Scandinavian block? Is Danish butter more English than Sherry or Port? If we want to buy a foreign car, do we think first of a Volvo or a Fiat? The Danish invasion of the ninth century was a particularly violent eruption of a volcano never totally quiescent.

CHAPTER THREE

Resistance and Death

It will be remembered that, according to Geoffrey, the primary reason for the election of Edmund to a restored East Anglian monarchy was to organize resistance against Danish piracy which was de-populating the coasts. From the complete silence of historians concerning any trouble in that area over the following decade, it can be presumed that he was fairly successful. Indeed, it is not impossible that his very success was the cause of a major military operation against him. It is a very different matter to organize local levies against a couple of boatloads of Vikings and to face a whole fleet carrying an army.

This occurred in 865, presumably in the late summer. It is at this point that the Bury Life becomes interesting. In spite of its late date, it gives details which are certainly correct and are not to be found elsewhere. For instance, it mentions Alfdene beside Hingwar and Ubba, along with other Danish chieftains, all with probable names. The army is stated to number 20,000: on the large side but not impossible. True, in the previous year the fleet is said to have attempted a landing in Scotland, which the historians reject; but, again, it is not impossible providing it was a failure. It seems certain that the primary object of the invasion was the conquest of Northumbria but, to do so, cavalry would be needed. It was impractical to bring horses across the North Sea. A landing should be attempted elsewhere in order to get the horses. There may well have been a probe to the north before settling for East Anglia.

Certain it is that the Danes landed like locusts in the Broads of East Anglia. Edmund's local levies were completely useless. All that could be done was to organize a resistance movement. We know a lot about these since the Hitler war; how damaging they can be, how difficult to suppress, but also how difficult to make effective. Edmund seems to have been excellent as a resistance leader. True, the Danes got the horses they needed and trained their cavalry throughout the winter but "every day lots of them were killed by the soldiers of St Edmund".

The obvious way to smash the resistance was to kill its leader. There seems to have been a deliberate hunt to catch the King. The

Bury Life provides a few examples, tall stories, doubtless, told in the Bury alehouses from generation to generation until they became history, only to be discredited by the historians. Here are some of them. The reader can take it for granted that none is historical fact although each is symbolically true.

Edmund was caught in a tower, a great round tower like the one at South Lopham perhaps. The besiegers and besieged were both reduced to starvation. Edmund ordered the last supply of corn to be fed to the remaining ox, which was then allowed to escape. The besiegers devoured the ox and, finding its stomach full of fresh corn knew the siege was useless, since the besieged could afford to feed their animals. The Danes turned tail. St Edmund and his companions mowed them down.

Then at Dernford, wherever that may be, he was completely surrounded but escaped miraculously by an unknown ford. Again, he was in a castle. A traitor told the Danes which part of the wall was weak; he knew because he had built it himself. Edmund, seeing all was lost, rushed out of the castle on horseback. On being stopped he said: "When I was in the Castle the King was still there". They let him go as an informer and so he escaped. Incidentally this story first appears in the Anglo-Norman poem of Gaimer of Troyes (c.1150) where it is inserted in St Edmund's Passion in 869. The Bury Life has clearly placed it in its proper place in 865/6. This surely shows that Bury must have possessed a source, now lost, older than the 12th century and more reliable than Gaimer.

Of course these stories are all alehouse stuff, but equally certainly they give a valuable picture of the war which was fought in 865/6: a war of "resistance" on the one side, of "hunt the leader" on the other.

It seems likely that the Hoxne legend belongs to this period. According to it, Edmund was being pursued by the Danes after the Battle of Thetford of 869. He hid under a bridge at Hoxne. Two lovers were not sufficiently absorbed to fail to notice the reflection of the king's golden spurs in the stream. They betrayed him. He was captured and killed. As it stands it is an unpleasant story: the disloyal lovers who betrayed their king. Originally it may have had a different ending: thanks to the lovers the king was saved. It would belong to the resistance war.

Then, suddenly in October 866, having trained their cavalry and stolen the harvest the Danes moved out to fulfil their intended task,

(i) Coronation of St Edmund. Manuscript 736 folio 8v—see page 8.

(ii) Left hand panel of Wilton Diptych showing Saints Edmund, Edward and John with Richard II.

(vii) Martyrdom of St Edmund. Manuscript 736 folio 14—see page 8.

Richard Burn, Sudbury.

(viii) Pew end in Hadleigh Church, Suffolk depicting wolf with head of St Edmund.

the conquest of Northumbria. York fell on November 1st. The rival kings of Northumbria, Osbert and Aelle, were both slain. There was no further resistance.

It is alarming to think on how delicate a thread civilisation hangs. Only a hundred years previously Northumbria was still at the apex of European culture. It had been the land of St Cuthbert, of the Venerable Bede, of St Hilda; in this very century it had known Alcuin teaching at York. All was wiped out like chalk on a blackboard. The fact is that the more advanced a civilisation the more it is vulnerable. Society becomes more complex and its members more interdependent. If one pillar of the edifice gives, the whole collapses. This applies, incidentally, as much to the England of today as to Northumbria in the ninth century. Of course there were those at the time who accepted the Danes as progressive: their unbelievable cruelty was realism; their debauchery humanism; their hatred of christianity liberalism; their contempt of culture individualism. There is never an "ism" lacking with which to destroy reality. Such was the end of one of the glories of these isles; Northumbria was no more.

The following year the Danes thought they might try their hand against Mercia. They captured Nottingham easily enough (which the Bury Life calls, so much more pleasantly, "Snottingham"). But then the tide began to turn. Burrhed, the King of Mercia, appealed to his brother-in-law of Wessex, Ethelred, who appeared with a large army and his younger brother Alfred—and, presumably, with Edmund of East Anglia. The presumption is by no means unwarranted because, as has already been said, on August 1st, 868, Burrhed signed a Charter in favour of Crowland Abbey at the instigation of Edmund and with Alfred as witness.

No battle seems to have been fought but the display of force was sufficient to make the Danes retire back to York, "where they spent the following year indulging their insane debaucheries and murdering men and women." (Bury Life).

Now it cannot really be supposed that between October, 866, when the Danes left East Anglia for York and November, 869, when they reappeared, Edmund had done absolutely nothing. It must at least have crossed his mind that a trained army would be a very useful thing. He seems to have formed one and to have attempted to give it the experience of hot war at the relief of Nottingham. Ingulf of Crowland, likely to be well informed, even credits Edmund with appointing a proper General, one Ulfketel. Hervey dismisses him as a confusion with the Earl Ufketel who fought so bravely along with Edmund Ironside against King Sweyn. But is it unknown to name a child after a distinguished ancestor, especially if that ancestor has so unusual a name as Ufketel? Anyway a very different reception was given to the Danes in 865 and 869. On their first arrival no more than a resistance movement was possible. On their second there was a pitched battle. The evidence for the pitched battle is overwhelming. The Anglo-Saxon Chronicle mentions it; Asser's Life of Alfred is explicit: "the heathen host marched through Mercia and East Anglia and set up winter quarters at a place called Thetford. That same year Edmund, King of the East Anglians, fought the said host *atrociter*—all out".

Much has been made of the fact that Abbo does not mention it, but, as had already been pointed out, apart from generalities, Abbo's text does not start until the day of the martyrdom, weeks later. It is Roger of Wendover who is responsible for interspersing the narrative of the campaign with speeches from Abbo. It enlivens the reading but is historically unsound.

A pitched battle there certainly was. It is not so easy to determine the campaign. The basic authorities contradict each other flatly: Asser and the Anglo-Saxon Chronicle say the Danes came by land; Abbo maintains they came by sea. Both must be right. Indeed, it is certain that the Danes avoided as far as possible allowing their land forces to get out of touch with their navy. If they did they would be liable to defeat. The cavalry and the light foot must have come by land; the supplies and engines of war by sea.

This is borne out by the places known to have been sacked by the Danes before the attack on East Anglia proper. The Bury Life gives the list: Crowland, Thorney, Peterborough, Ramsey, Soham and Ely. Crowland and Ely were on islands that could only be attacked with ships. Thorney, Peterborough and Ramsey were on the mainland, albeit on navigable waterways, and could be stormed by land. Soham probably plays a different part.

What appears to have happened is that Hingwar appeared with the land forces on the chalk escarpment near Newmarket while Ubba with the supplies was sacking Ely. The obvious place to defend East Anglia was on the escarpment at Devil's Dyke. But this was impossible because Ubba had already out-flanked the English or was threatening to do so by landing from Ely at Soham. Hence there was nothing for it but to make a stand further inland. Hingwar pushed through to

Thetford. That was where the battle was joined. It is said to have lasted the whole day and the carnage was terrific. Poor Ulfketel, if he ever existed, ceased to do so. Edmund survived. He seems, indeed, to have had the better of the battle, since he was able to give decent burial to his dead and to have wept over the corpses of the Danes, whose souls were irremediably damned. Ecumenicity was not fashionable in the ninth century. Edmund must have been in possession of the battlefield.

It must have been at this point that Ubba turned up from Soham. He had presumably re-embarked on discovering that there was to be no battle at Devil's Dyke and had come up the river Thet. It put Edmund in a difficult position. Could his army stand another pitched battle against a freshly reinforced foe?

What happened? Did he simply retire north to Hellesdon? Was there another pitched battle in which Edmund's army was wiped out? Was there some sort of treaty? None can say but, in the light of future events, the last alternative seems the most probable. How much time elapsed between the battle of Thetford and the martyrdom on November the 20th? Again one simply does not know.

Before proceeding further it must be admitted with the greatest regret that Hellesdon, on the north-west outskirts of Norwich, not Hoxne in Suffolk, is the place of the martyrdom. The evidence of Abbo is conclusive. Lord Francis Hervey points out as well that in the will of Bishop Theodred, a great devotee of St Edmund, in about 950, Hoxne is mentioned as having a church dedicated to St Ethelbert the Martyr, but there is no allusion to St Edmund. Lord Francis proceeds to make a bold claim for Hollesley Bay, but it is as imaginative as ingenious. Hellesdon it is.

But what is Edmund doing at Hellesdon? Where has his army gone? He seems only to have had Bishop Humbert, a few chaplains, and a small bodyguard in attendance. He must have thought himself perfectly safe. Why didn't he escape to the Marshlands, not a day's ride away, where his predecessors had held out against all the might of Mercia and Wessex? Could he not have rekindled the resistance movement which he had led so successfully a few years before? Such questions require answers but they are not easily given. All one can do is to examine the text of the eye-witness account.

Apart from the mention of Hellesdon in Chapter VI, this starts at Chapter VII of Abbo's work.

VII. A Danish messenger arrives completely unexpectedly, *inprovisum*. Hingwar is said to be following leisurely behind. He delivers his message to the unsuspecting king, *incautum*. Edmund is required to share his "family treasures and inheritance and to rule under Hingwar as a subject King—*sub eo regnaturus*". There follows the appropriate threats.

VIII. His Bishop (Humbert) advises Edmund to comply. Edmund's answer is not without nobility, and rings true: "my dear Bishop, we have arrived at a point in life which we could never have conceived. The sword of a foreign savage is held at the throat of the natives of our land. Our groaning people, once so care-free, with a gasp fall silent. If only those who now creep around in fear of their lives could be spared by my death and so survive to live on in their beloved land, then in due course all would be restored to its former happiness."

The attitude seems genuine enough. The idea of martyrdom is still distant although not absent: if only he could die for his people!

The Bishop then advises flight. It would surely have been easy.

But the King has become fascinated with the idea of dying for his people. Abbo gives him a long speech, full, alas! of classical clichés but psychologically sound. Why should he flee? Why should he survive his people? Never has he been a traitor yet. Then, the religious twist comes in quite naturally: "the Almighty, the Judge of all things, is my witness that, living or dead, nothing will separate me from the love of Christ to whom I was wedded in the bond of faith by baptism, when I renounced Satan and all his pomps. And indeed it so happens that, to the praise and glory of the Blessed Trinity, I have thrice received the holy oil of Chrism: at baptism, at confirmation, and upon my coronation." He had accepted the yoke of Christ; he would accept none other.

IX. This long chapter of over 500 words contains nothing bnt Edmund's answer to the messenger. It can be summed up in its last few lines: "hence you must know that I will not submit to a pagan master for the love of earthly life; first you must join our holy religion. King Edmund, the Christian, prefers to hold his banner high in the court of the Eternal King."

There are some 200 words in the middle of the text which certainly must have puzzled Edmund's armour-bearer. They are in fact a learned discourse on the difference between free and forced contracts. He who accepts a forced contract is nothing but a slave. It ends up with the following: "so, as everybody knows who has had to administer justice (both Edmund and Hingwar, after all, were kings), the immediate result of forced contracts, as far as free human acts are concerned, is that it is the tyrant who suffers—from his loss of self-respect."

Of course it may all be Dunstan or Abbo giving a little lesson in political ethics. But if there is a basis of historical fact behind the lecture, it looks very much as though there had been a free treaty between Edmund and Hingwar, about which of course the armour-bearer knew nothing, and which was now being broken. Dunstan failed to understand what his witness was getting at and inserted an appropriate lecture instead.

It is very suggestive. The breaking of a solemn treaty would explain why the messenger came "unexpectedly" and why Edmund was "unsuspecting". It would also explain, later, the extraordinary reaction of the Danes.

X. The messenger returns to Hingwar who by now is in the neighbourhood. He orders the place to be surrounded and Edmund alone to be killed. Edmund was chained, beaten, tied to a tree and lashed. "But he was not broken, the whole time he muttered with a feeble voice the holy name of Jesus Christ." This annoyed his persecutors who started shooting arrows at him, but not so as to kill him. At last Hingwar ordered his head, still uttering the Holy Name, to be cut off. This was on November 20th, 869.

So died St Edmund. As he stood there, muttering the Holy Name, he must have thought what a failure he had been. Things were not too bad when he had taken over his little kingdom: a bit disorderly perhaps, but quite tolerable. Look at it now! It had been a hard struggle to preserve civilised standards, to encourage the rudiments of culture, to further education. He might as well not have tried! To administer justice and to protect the realm, that was what a king was there for. The foreign savage had put an end to them. Then there was his religion, dearer to him than himself. Would it even survive? He might call on the Holy Name, but who else would, once his voice was silent? Even his dear old Bishop Humbert had advised him to compromise. It was one of the things which amused him about the clergy: so firm on the moral law and so lacking in moral courage. For all his trimming, the poor old bishop was in for a rough time. Iesu! . . . . How lucky he hadn't married; at least only he was suffering, Iesu! . . Am I dying correctly? Is that how it should be done? Iesu! Iesu! Anyway, I preserved my own integrity, Iesu! My integrity, what does that matter! Iesu! I have attempted to preserve the honour of . . . . Iesu!

CHAPTER FOUR

Here! Here! Here!

Normally, once the hero is dead the story of his body comes to an end. One can discuss his ideas, his influence, even at a pinch the chances of his eternal salvation, but his body has been happily disposed of in the grave. Not so with Edmund. His body has a vastly longer and more curious history after death than it had in life. This new story starts off straight away on November 20th, 869.

The mutilated body was left lying where it was, but the head was taken away and thrown in the deepest thicket of the neighbouring forest. Now, it is one thing to collect heads but quite another to throw them away. Some explanation is needed. Abbo gives one: to prevent decent burial. But it doesn't work. Such minor details did not worry the Danes. Anyway they could have burnt the body or cut it up and thrown it to the dogs.

What normally induces people to carry heads away with them? The usual motive, presumably, is to prove that the right person has been murdered. But Hingwar himself was present; he had no need of proof.

For some reason unknown to us did Hingwar wish the body to be un-identified and the murder unknown, at least immediately? But merely to remove the head would be inadequate for such a purpose.

The most reasonable solution, surely, is that Hingwar changed his mind. He took the head for the perfectly normal purpose of sticking it on the end of a pole to terrorise the English. Perhaps he had already done so before he had left Hellesdon and the head was carried before him as he returned leisurely to camp. But he couldn't look at it. He had witnessed the martyrdom. Even he was overcome. Throw it away! Deep in the woods so that it is never seen again! That head which kept muttering Iesu!

Hingwar died within the twelve-month and not, as he would have wished, in battle. It is just possible that he died of a broken conscience.

Such are the facts, construe them as one may. It looks strangely as though St Edmund's first miracle occurred on the day and at the scene of his martyrdom: Hingwar's change of heart.

The English recovered his body all right. But what had happened to the head? Hingwar failed to parade it, so it must have been thrown away. But where? A methodical hunt was organized through the forest, along the road by which Hingwar had left. The searchers were stretched over a wide area, but in earshot of each other, so as to ensure covering the suspected ground. From the depth of a thicket they heard a voice crying: "Here, here, here." They penetrated the spot and there was the dead head crying out between the paws of a great wolf.

There may be a little over-statement in the story. The *lupus*, the wolf, is likely to have been the king's own wolfhound, whose great bark, rather than the dead head, supplied the Here, here, here, sound. But the basic story must be accepted. The searchers carried the head to where the body lay, placed the two parts together, presumably laid the relic of the True Cross on the King's breast and placed it all in a decent coffin. They carried it to a neighbouring village, which Hermann calls Sutton. They laid the coffin on the ground with a respectable covering over it and built a make-shift chapel.

It is comforting to discover that not only in the twentieth century do temporary buildings tend to become permanent. The makeshift chapel at Sutton by Hellesdon must have remained the shrine of St Edmund for several years.

Precisely at the time when the shrine was most neglected Edmund's fame spread most rapidly. There can be little doubt but that his greatest miracle was to draw the English together. The two kings of Northumbria had died honourably in battle: nobody seemed to care. The King of little East Anglia was martyred and the country was electrified. There is no denying that English resistance to the pagan invasion stiffened almost miraculously after Edmund's death. It is certain that Alfred was the human cause; it is equally certain that Edmund was Alfred's inspiration. When Alfred first minted coins in Edmund's honour cannot be known but there is no reason why he should not have done so upon his accession in 871. He obviously intended that the martyred King should be a lesson and example to the men of England. His memory was to be kept fresh. The result was simply astonishing. Within a decade Hingwar's successor, Guthrum, had become a Christian by the pact of Chippenham in 878.

As though that were not enough, there is the miracle of the Danish reaction, which had started perhaps in the heart of Hingwar himself, when he threw the head away. The Danes, too, minted coins in

Edmund's honour. They too proclaimed his sanctity. There is a clear intention "to make an act of reparation in him and through him". It is a most extraordinary story. This man who had appeared a complete failure turned out to be the creator of English unity. It is perhaps not unfitting at this juncture to quote from William of Malmesbury: "It is an auspicious circumstance that the first place in my narrative should be occupied by St Edmund, who as a patriot prince and King challenges the first right to the palm of glory among his sainted fellow countrymen."

Apart from the miracle of national unity, little private miracles, divine interventions in the details of personal lives, were multiplying around the tomb. Abbo mentions the fact, but gives no examples. The reason for this is not far to seek: after the burial of St Edmund the armour-bearer ceases to be an eye-witness of what he had to say. Dunstan did not wish to weaken the force of his narrative by including miraculous hearsay. Incidentally, from this point onwards, there is some difficulty in fixing Abbo's chronology: the armour-bearer reported what he knew but was not always certain of when it happened.

One has to wait another hundred years to find, in William of Malmesbury, the first recorded miracle at St Edmund's lowly shrine. This is the account given later still (c.1180) by Abbot Samson.

"A certain blind man and the lad who led him had lost their way .. the sun set; the darkness thickened. They grew frightened. No house was to be seen; wild animals made it dangerous to rest beneath a tree. Suddenly the lad spots a house: 'Hurrah!' he shouts, 'it is a tiny hut, but will do in our present plight' .... They go in and knock against the Martyr's tomb. They guess it to be a place of human burial and at first are horror-struck. However, necessity gives them courage and they lay down with the tomb as pillow. Scarcely had they laid them down to sleep when a column of light, like a flame, fills the place .... The lad wakes his master, crying out 'Up, up, master! our house is on fire!' But the blind man, moved by some interior presentiment, calmed the lad: 'Be quiet,' he says; 'don't worry. Our host tonight is faithful and true. We shall suffer no harm. Sleep peacefully'.... Dawn broke. ... The blind man said to his lad: 'It is growing light; let us be on our way.' 'And how can you tell it is light when others have to tell you? Can you see or are you mad?' 'You don't think I am fooling you,' the old man replied; 'What I said last night has been confirmed by reality; our host is faithful and true' ...."

Quite apart from charm, the story illustrates well enough St Edmund's first burial place. The body was laid on the ground—"requievit humatus" in the words of Abbo. It was covered with what Abbo calls "a decent mausoleum", a lowish wooden structure which at a pinch could be used as a head-rest for tramps. Over this was built a wretched little chapel no better than a hut.

But, if the shrine was crude, St Edmund did not lack the devotion of the faithful. From a careful reading of Abbo, it is clear that the extraordinary story of the holy woman, Oswen, belongs to this period although he happens to refer to it after the removal of the body to Boedericsworth, later Bury St Edmunds. This good woman constituted herself the guardian of the tomb. It clearly must have been she who first discovered that the body was incorrupt, because, every Maundy Thursday, she used to lift up the covering of the corpse and cut the hair and nails! These she carefully collected in a casket, which was eventually hung over the shrine at Bury, where it remained intact until the Dissolution. It is obvious that the hair and nails would continue to grow for a short time after death on an incorrupt body but would eventually stop doing so. They would scarcely start growing only when the corpse arrived at Boedericsworth. Moreover, when the body was brought to this town, it was put into the custody of secular priests who would certainly not have allowed poor Oswen to perform her ministrations.

And how long did the body remain in the hut at Sutton? Abbo says "for many years", which might mean three or four. Archdeacon Hermann gave a minimum of 56 years since he places the translation to Boedericsworth in the reign of King Athelstan of England (925 - 941). He is most circumstantial and gives the names of the original guardians into whose hands the relics were placed. The Bury Life mentions 33 years for no very obvious reason. What is likely to be true?

Surely it springs immediately to the eye that Hermann is in possession of the facts but has misidentified the Athelstan. The translation took place not in the reign of Athelstan of England but of Athelstan II Guthrum of East Anglia. That is, between his conversion in 878 and his death in 890. As has already been pointed out, this King was minting money in the name of Eadmond, which may well be commemorative coinage of the translation. Moreover, St Edmund was the symbol of the "act of reparation" of the pagan Danes to the Christian English. Also, the Pope was badgering Alfred to hasten the conversion of the Danes. In such circumstances it is surely unlikely that Athelstan II Guthrum should have left St Edmund's remains in a miserable hut in some remote forest.

An early date for the translation, say 880, also fits in with Oswen. Edmund was put to earth (humatus) at the end of November 869. She jealously guards the tomb. Comes Holy Week, 870, the Passion of Our Lord makes her meditate on the passion of her hero. By the evening of Maundy Thursday her devotion and curiosity combined become irresistible. Just a peep at the dear remains! Good Heavens, the body is incorrupt! But he is no longer the beautiful young man she had seen in life but has grown a massive beard and great, gnarled nails. Piously she restores him. She is, of course, immensely discreet, but the story gets round. On Maundy Thursday, 871, there is a local pilgrimage; no priests, naturally, partly because there are not any, partly because they are always preaching against superstition. This can go on as a popular devotion as opposed to an ecclesiastical pilgrimage until the apparently miraculous conversion of the pagan King in 878. Then there is the triumph! On Maundy Thursday, 879, Guthrum, now Athelstan II, was invited to turn up. Doubtless he refused owing to previous engagements but the clergy poked their noses in. Yes, the body was incorrupt. Order must immediately be introduced to prevent superstition. The body will be translated to Boedericsworth and placed under the care of reliable ecclesiastics. That is what would happen. That, then, is what did happen. Poor Oswen came too. She could fast and pray as much as she liked but her care of the corpse was no longer required. They paid her off by placing her casket of hair and nails for all to see over the high altar.

There is striking corroboration in favour of the translation taking place in Guthrum's reign from the Chronicle of Jocelin. In 1198 the Saint's coffin was found to have iron rings at either end, "as there used to be in Danish chests". Edmund was certainly not put into a fine coffin, with iron handles after the Danish manner, at his hasty burial by the English in 869. He would only acquire a proper, solid coffin when the body had to be transported all the way from Hellesdon to Boedericsworth. To Jocelin's unbiased eye this coffin appeared to be of Danish manufacture. The only likely date for it is in the reign of Athelstan II Guthrum.

There is a further reason for placing the translation of the relics to Boedericsworth in or around 880: the relics were certainly verified by Bishop Theodred (926 - 951), presumably before 929, the probable date of Athelstan's visit. He would certainly not have verified a relic that had already been authenticated in living memory, or even, according to Hermann, the previous year.

Lastly, according to Abbo it was at the time of the translation that Edmund was canonised. This also places the translation into the reign of Athelstan II Guthrum, since, as has already been said, coins unquestionably struck before 890 style him "Sc Eadmund Rex".

At the translation one extraordinary phenomenen was verified: the severed head had re-attached itself to the body. Only a thin red crease remained to show where it had been cut off. This was attested not only by Oswen but also by the ecclesiastical authorities who supervised the translation. Presumably Edmund's skin, like his hair and nails, continued to grow quite abnormally after death.

The relics were carried with great pomp to an enormous church, wonderfully constructed of wood, at Boedericsworth. Nothing, of course, of this church remains, but there is no reason to doubt its splendour. After all, St Dunstan and Abbo did not have to rely on the armour-bearer's evidence for this assertion; they had seen it themselves. One can get some idea of the innate skill of the East Anglians in wood from the wonderful examples of a later date still scattered around the province. The roof of Needham Market Church must be unique in England as is the wooden octagon of Ely. The roofs of St Mary's at Bury or at Wymondham Abbey are larger but no finer than those in countless humble churches. Screens of untold beauty are dotted all over Norfolk and Suffolk. The absence of any local stone, apart from flint, forced the East Anglians to cultivate the art of building in wood. Apparently they did St Edmund proud.

It is probably at this juncture, having described the death of his hero, established his incorruptibility, proclaimed his canonisation and translated his relics to Boedericsworth, that the narrative of the armour-bearer originally stopped. Abbo gives Bishop Theodred himself as the source of the next chapter, XVI.

Theodred was Bishop of Elmham from 926 to 951. The event must have occurred at the start of his episcopate, partly because he was clearly inexperienced in wielding power, partly because he is said to have regretted his action "for the rest of his life", as though he lived for many years after. Besides, if St Dunstan heard it from his own lips in 929, the event must have occurred before that date, say 927.

This is the story. Many rich gifts of gold and silver had been presented to the shrine. A band of eight thieves decided to loot it. They started out on their enterprise. One had a ladder to get through a window, another a crowbar to break the bars and bolts; others brought picks and shovels to undermine a point in the wall. Suddenly they were literally petrified with fear. They remained motionless in the very act of attempting sacrilege. Thus were they caught redhanded on the following morning. They were brought before Theodred, who ordered them to be hanged.

It is at this point that the story becomes interesting. The Bishop was overwhelmed with remorse at the harshness of his own sentence. He inflicted a severe penance on himself, which was fair enough. When this was finished, he imposed a three-day fast on the whole of the Diocese, which seems a bit unfair; and wound the business up by convening everybody to be present while he transferred the body of St Edmund from the old shrine (mausoleum) in which it had been brought from Sutton to a new one. And so it was done. In front of all the people, the body was found whole and incorrupt. The Bishop handled it, washed it, clothed it afresh and placed it in a new shrine.

It is now about sixty years since the martyrdom. While at Sutton the body had been seen each Maundy Thursday by Oswen; it was officially examined somewhere around 880 and translated to Bury when Edmund was canonised. Again, around 927, the body was found incorrupt and placed in a new shrine. No wonder the martyr King became famous throughout the land!

Abbo's account ends with a story which it is impossible to date. Its source cannot be the armour-bearer and is not Bishop Theodred. It may well have occurred many years after 929, and is not part of St Dunstan's original version. Abbo introduces it apologetically in Chapter XVII; "I hope I shall not bore the reader by telling of a certain fellow .... ". He is clearly telling the story off his own authority, as he could scarcely accuse Dunstan of boring anyone. The event must therefore have occurred after 929 but before Abbo wrote in 985. Let us put it half-way, say about 960.

The certain fellow was one Leofstan. He was young, of noble birth and wielded immense power in the province. His father was a pious old man called Aelfgar. This arrogant youth wanted to have a look at St Edmund. His servants tried to dissuade him, but he insisted. The shrine was duly opened; he looked in. At the same moment he went mad. His father disinherited him. He died in poverty, riddled with worms. That was the end of Leofstan. But he provided another verification of the presence of St Edmund's incorrupt body towards the middle of the tenth century.

CHAPTER FIVE

The Monk Ailwin

Life ran reasonably smoothly at Boedericsworth in the second half of the tenth century. Pilgrimages to the shrine of St Edmund increased and consequently the revenue at the disposal of the guardians, who numbered no fewer than twenty priests and had constituted themselves into a college of secular canons. They were doubtless perfectly decent men but, as the money rolled in, the zeal ebbed out. In 990 the Bishop, another Athelstan, was sufficiently disedified by them to put a Benedictine monk from St Benet's Hulme in Norfolk in charge of the relics. His name was Ailwin, alias Aegelwin. Incidentally, Hulme must be amongst the most forlorn ruins in East Anglia. An arch amongst the reeds and willows is all that remains of this once famous Abbey.

Ailwin was a most extraordinary man. Born of pious and wealthy parents, he showed all the virtues one expects but does not always get in the educated classes. He was loyal, devout, courageous, determined, independent. In the difficult years ahead, God's divine providence had arranged for the right man to be in charge.

Since he had been made responsible for an incorrupt body, the first thing he did was to have a look at it. He found that it needed a wash and the hair, unkempt since Oswen's day, needed combing. He did it at regular intervals. Any hair which came off from the comb, he placed with Oswen's clippings and parings. This went on peacefully for a number of years, although already in 994 there was a warning of what was to come: in that year King Sweyn of Denmark made his first invasion. Concerning Sweyn, his character can best be judged by the fact that he murdered his own father, Harold Blodrand, to obtain the crown. Not a pleasant type.

The political history of the next fifteen years is outside the scope of the present study. Suffice it to say that the English King, Ethelred, was not only ill-counselled but also a coward. On St Brice's Day, November 13th, 1003, there was a general massacre of Danes in England; not a proud day in our annals. Luckily, Sweyn's ablest general, Count Turchil defected to the English in 1009. It is an unpleasant page in history, where folly and cowardice are mitigated by greed and treason.

In all this turmoil, what was Ailwin to do with his precious relic? Not only was Bury very exposed, but Sweyn could be expected to bear a particular grudge against St Edmund both as patron of the English and as the symbol of Danish appeasement in the previous century. He decided that the safest place was London. He constructed a litter on wheels, a sort of glorified pram, and with a few companions wheeled the body to London by devious routes to avoid the Danes. There was plenty of excitement on the way but, thanks to plenty of miracles, he managed to get through.

The arrival in London seems to have been a triumph. Ailwin approached the City from Stamford. Unfortunately he was baulked by the swollen River Lea. The ford was unpassable and the footbridge too narrow for the litter. There was Ailwin, stuck within sight of St Paul's! Dauntless, however, he pushed on. With one wheel on the plank and the other suspended in mid-air, the litter gained the London bank. Somewhat naturally, after so unusual an entry, the populace gathered to accompany the relics to St Paul's. But the Monk Ailwin was a shrewd man and well acquainted with the acquisitive instincts of bishops. He knew that if once his precious relic ever got into St Paul's it would never come out again, so he made for the little church of St Gregory the Great, in the shadow of the Cathedral. There the relics remained for three years with Ailwin hovering over them like a hawk.

It must have been very soon after the arrival in London that Elphege, Archbishop of Canterbury, tried to buy from Ailwin the relic of the True Cross which hung around Edmund's neck, because he was at Canterbury throughout the early months of 1011 until he was captured by the Danes on September 20th and martyred on the following April 12th. Ailwin, of course, refused this sacriligeous offer: relics are not for sale. The incident is interesting as it provides the first mention of the relic. It is perfectly clear that it had not been added to the corpse after death and, as has been seen, it supplies a valuable clue to the origins of St Edmund himself. It is also interesting to note Elphege's priorities; he was willing to pay a large sum for a relic, which was quite wrong of him; he was killed for refusing to be ransomed because of the burden it would impose on his flock, although he could licitly have done so. Truly a great man!

There can be no doubt, of course, but that the three years in London contributed largely to St Edmund's fame. Although Alfred had proclaimed him a national hero, by force of circumstance he had remained a local East Anglian Saint. Once in the Capital, however, he did really become a national hero, the symbol of resistance, such as Alfred had intended him to be. It is noteworthy that Count Turchil was converted to Christianity and renounced his allegiance to Sweyn in 1012, precisely when St Edmund was also in the City. It is certain that this Danish general who saved London from the Danes prayed beside the relics of our Saint.

Early in 1013 Ailwin decided to bring the relics back to Bury. Obviously he did not know that Sweyn was preparing his third and most formidable invasion, but he might have guessed it. The truth probably is that between the two evils of Alphun, Bishop of London, grabbing the relics as he was constantly trying to do, and a further Danish invasion, the latter was the less dangerous. Ailwin might be able to cope with the Danes but not with the Bishop.

Anyway, after a final and unsuccessful attempt by Alphun to steal the relics, Ailwin started on his way back to Bury. He took the old main road through Edmunton, which still bears his name, to Chipping Ongar, near which at Greenstead the remarkable wooden church, in which the body rested, is still standing. Then through Chelmsford, Braintree, and Clare to Boedericsworth.

He could scarcely have arrived home when Sweyn landed. Apart from the Dane, Turchil, the English put up little resistance. Even Winchester fell without a blow. In January 1014 the wretched Ethelred fled to Normandy. It seemed the end of England.

As a matter of fact, Sweyn had not plundered and sacked Boedericsworth. He was far too busy. However, quite naturally from his point of view, when he decided to ransom England by the levy of a prodigious tax, he did not exclude the untaxable "patrimony of St Edmund", still comparatively small. It was not the money which upset Ailwin: after all he didn't touch it; it went to the maintenance of the shrine and the support of the canons, whereas he was a monk of Hulme. No, it was the principle of the thing. Sweyn was supposed to be a Christian, albeit only in name, and should know better. Ailwin hesitated: if he refused he knew the consequences; but to comply seemed dishonourable. He was on the verge of complying when he had a vision. St Edmund appeared to him: "go and deliver my message to King Sweyn", said Edmund. "Ask him in my name: why do you tax the people who pay tribute to none but me? ... I am a terrible protector of my own".

One can jeer of course. Monkish over-wroughtness! But the fact is there: Ailwin did precisely that. It must be among the most extraordinary acts of moral and physical courage in English history: this comic monk from Boedericsworth goes all the way to Gainsborough, where Sweyn had established his capital, to tell the most ruthless monarch in the history of western Europe, the assassin of his own father and the plunderer of England, that a fellow who had died a failure nearly 150 years before was "a terrible protector of his own". It is past belief in heroism or folly but it happens to be true.

Ailwin arrived at Gainsborough on February 1st, 1014. He delivered his message. Sweyn heard him, cursed him for a fool and sent him packing: he wasn't worth killing. Disconsolate, Ailwin trundled back to Lincoln on his way home. He arrived there on the evening of February 2nd. That night Sweyn died. It was a sudden but tormented death. In his delirium he kept on shouting that Edmund had struck him. Anyway he died. The man who had held all England in his grasp was placed in a narrow coffin and shipped to Denmark for his burial. Ailwin returned to Boedericsworth to guard his precious corpse.

There it is. It does not much matter if people of today believe it or not, because the one man who really mattered seems to have believed it. Sweyn's son and heir, King Cnut.

This astonishing story has been told at some length for two reasons. The first is to perpetuate the memory of the monk Ailwin: moral and physical courage are rarely combined in the same person. A man may win the V.C. but be terrified to question a bill in a restaurant: a woman may raise a prodigious row over the bill but jump on a chair at the sight of a mouse. Ailwin questioned the bill and faced the monarch. The second reason is to explain the extraordinary solicitude of Cnut for the shrine of St Edmund.

With the example of the monk Ailwin before him, Cnut decided to get rid of the secular canons as the guardians of the shrine and found a great Benedictine Abbey at Boedericsworth. The Benedictines accordingly moved in in 1020 under Abbot Uvius, alias Aelfric, Prior of Hulme. It is from now onwards that the town came to be called the borough of St Edmund instead of Boedericsworth. The following year Ailwin was made Bishop of Elmham.

Such, at least, is Hermann's story—but it is very unlikely to be true. Events must have occurred the other way round. Ailwin was appointed Bishop in 1021 all right. Instead of going to Elmham and leaving the body which he had guarded for thirty years of his life, he transferred the See to Boedericsworth which he renamed the Borough of St Edmund. He dismissed the secular canons and imported the

Benedictines from his own abbey of Hulme. In fact, Bury became the centre of the diocese with the Cathedral served by Benedictines, just like Canterbury and, later, Norwich. Either Hermann is deceiving deliberately or his text has been falsified to lend support to the claim by the abbey of freedom from episcopal jurisdiction, during the quarrel between Bishop Herfast and Abbot Baldwin in 1070—of which more anon.

The new Abbey was royally endowed. A grant of fourpence a year on each carucate of land was to be paid to St Edmund in perpetuity from all over East Anglia. As a matter of fact, however, the Abbey did not enjoy this revenue for long, as Herbert de Losinga got it transferred to him in 1096 to pay for the building of Norwich Cathedral. Queen Emma gave the Abbey all her possessions in Suffolk, except for the Castles of Eye and Clare. This gift created the County of West Suffolk much as we know it today.

The first care of the Benedictines was to build an abbey church in stone. This was a long and costly process. It was not consecrated until October 18th, 1032. The body of St Edmund was transferred with great pomp to the new shrine. Cnut was there and so also, most probably, Turchil, who had become the Earl of East Anglia. Cnut placed his crown upon the high altar and redeemed it with a splendid gift. Ailwin was also present. He was very old by now and totally blind. According to Hermann, he was asked by the Abbot (but was he?) to verify that the body was exactly as he had left it. Since he could not see, he did so by touch: "Ægelwin feels it with his hands and finds all inside (the coffin) as he had left it, notably the reliquary of the Lord's Cross (scilicet Crucis Dominicae philaterium) hanging from his neck on the Saint's breast. Archbishop Ælfeg, the Martyr, some time back in London had wanted to buy it for a great weight of gold but could not, even had he offered all the gold in Tharsis, because of Aegelwin, the Martyr's guardian." (Hermann).

It is a moving picture: the blind old bishop feeling the face he had so often washed, running his fingers through the hair he had combed, touching the little reliquary which he has managed to save. He placed on the coffin some poems in honour of St. Edmund written in Anglo-Saxon, the text of which is, alas! lost. He must have been a very happy old man when he died a few years later.

The passage is also important because it establishes beyond any doubt the presence of the relic of the True Cross. It cannot have been a mere crucifix, not only because Archbishop Elphege would not have offered a great weight of gold for it, but also because "philaterium" means reliquary, as Archdeacon Hermann knew perfectly well since, in another passage, he calls the cupboard containing the reliquaries the "servatorium cum phylacteriis".

It should be noted that Hermann does not mention the building of Cnut's church in 1032 and the consequent verification of the body. He is therefore led to place the events of 1032 as though they happened in 1050. This has led both Mackinlay and Bordier to suppose that Ailwin was present at the verification of 1050. But he cannot have been. When Ailwin was present, everything was left as it was and he himself replaced the lid of the coffin: but in 1050 the body was stripped of its clothing. Moreover, Ailwin cannot have been under thirty years of age when he was appointed guardian of the relics in 990. This would make him over 90 in 1050, an unlikely age for travel in those days. In fact Ailwin probably died shortly after his retirement from the Bishopric, in about 1035. But did he even retire? We only have Hermann's dubious word for it. He probably died in office. His immediate successor was Bishop Ælfric II, whose date of consecration is uncertain and who in turn was succeeded by Ælfric III, certainly consecrated in 1039.

Order is restored to Hermann's narrative by putting all that concerns Ailwin into the opening of the stone church in 1032. Hermann's chronology has already been found doubtful when he placed the removal of St Edmund to Boedericsworth after 925 instead of before 890. But there may be a reason for Hermann's mistake. When he was writing, Abbot Baldwin of Bury was claiming independence for the Abbey from episcopal jurisdiction, as has been mentioned. But if Bishop Ailwin verified the body in 1032 it would be clear that the Abbey was subject to the bishop. Hence Ailwin was resuscitated to be a mere witness of the verification of 1050, by which time he would not be exercising episcopal jurisdiction even if he were alive. It is, in fact, a repetition of Hermann's falsification concerning the introduction of the Benedictines.

As has been mentioned, only eighteen years passed between the construction of Cnut's church and a further verification of the relics. It is in every respect a strange tale. A woman, whose parents had given her the unprepossessing name of Ælfgeth, was dumb. She came from Winchester on a pilgrimage to Bury St Edmunds where she gradually recovered her speech. In gratitude she stayed on and made herself useful by scrubbing the floor of the church and arranging the flowers. One night St Edmund appeared to her and told her to inform the authorities that his body was in a shocking state: woodworm had got into the lid of his coffin and he was being showered with wood dust; spiders were weaving their webs all over his face. Something should be done about it.

The Abbot, Leofstan, thought the woman mad and did nothing. However, Ælfgeth went on having her visions and importuned the Abbot until he finally gave in. Under the wood dust and cobwebs the body was found to be perfect. It was exposed on a table for all to see. It exhaled a wonderful perfume. Apparently, when Bishop Theodred had stripped, washed and re-clothed the body in 927, he had piously replaced the original shirt, blood-stained and tattered by the arrows. This was now removed and a new shirt put on. The old one was placed in the cupboard for relics.

Before the body was replaced in the coffin an extraordinary event happened. Abbot Leofstan, on a sudden impulse, decided to verify whether the head was really attached to the body. He called on a young monk to hold the saint's feet whilst he tugged at the head. At that precise moment he had a stroke. He pulled so hard that he dragged the body and the young monk with it; presumably they all collapsed together on the floor. The head was certainly firmly rooted to the body. It must have been an immensely grim sight. Anyway, Leofstan was dumb, blind and paralysed in his arms as a result. Edward the Confessor was informed, who immediately despatched his personal physician, one Baldwin, a Frenchman born at Chartres and a Benedictine monk of St Denis near Paris. Either through Baldwin's ministrations or through the passage of time, Leofstan regained his sight and speech but his hands remained paralysed for the rest of his life. Baldwin was so impressed both by the event and by the abbey that he transferred from St Denis to Bury St Edmunds and became Leofstan's successor as Abbot in 1065.

Before leaving the verification of the relics of 1050 one little detail must be rectified. Mackinlay says that "the relic of the True Cross was not replaced in the coffin along with St Edmund". It was. Mackinlay's error comes from a hasty reading of Hermann. Here is the text: "Exuviae vero martyris in servatorio reconduntur cum phylacteriis". This Mackinlay presumably took to mean: the strippings of the body (the exuviae, i.e. the blood-stained shirt) along with the reliquaries (cum phylacteriis, i.e. the True Cross) were placed in a cupboard. But that surely is not what Hermann means, which is: the strippings off the Martyr's body were placed in the cupboard containing the reliquaries. It is only the shirt which was removed. Ailwin's salutations in Anglo-Saxon and the Cross remained.

Incidentally it is the same Abbot Leofstan who brought back to Bury from Lucca, which he visited on his way to Rome, a copy of the Volto Santo. The Volto Santo is an early and splendid representation of the Crucifixion still venerated in Lucca. The copy given to Leofstan must have been the most outstanding work of art in Bury Abbey. Lucca in the eleventh and twelfth centuries was at the height of its political power and artistic achievement. The copy was eventually placed in the Chapel of the Holy Cross at Bury where it remained until the Dissolution, when we shall hear more about it.

CHAPTER SIX

From Baldwin to Samson

Now let us return to Abbot Baldwin. Bury was singularly fortunate to have such an Abbot at the time of the Norman conquest. When William the Conqueror was busy filling bishoprics and abbeys with his nominees Bury remained unmolested. Unfortunately in 1070 William placed one of his chaplains, Herfast, on the East Anglian See. This prelate moved to Thetford, presumably to keep an eye on Bury, over which he claimed episcopal jurisdiction. As a matter of fact he was almost certainly right. As has been seen, it is most unlikely that the Benedictines had been brought to Bury by any other than Bishop Ailwin. The same Bishop conducted a canonical verification of the relics in 1032 while exercising episcopal authority. He was not a witness in 1050, because more likely than not he was dead. Moreover, the unbelievable generosity of Bury in handing over to Bishop Herbert De Losinga, in 1096, the fourpence tax on each carugate of land, granted by Cnut, can only be explained as a payment to settle the dispute. However, episcopal supervision did not matter much with easygoing English bishops, but it was a very different story with a competent, interfering Norman on your doorstep. As soon as Herfast was appointed, in 1070-1071 Baldwin set out for Rome to claim that Bury was exempt from episcopal jurisdiction and depended directly on the Holy See. Right or more probably wrong, of course Baldwin got his way, for the lasting good of the Abbey.

Upon his return to Bury, Baldwin set about erecting the great Abbey Church which survived until the Dissolution in 1539. At its consecration on Sunday, April 29th, 1095, it was certainly the largest and finest building in England and indeed among the finest in Christendom. Alas! the few bits of rubble which remain scarcely give any idea of it. Its facade was as wide and imposing as Lincoln; its nave was as majestic as Ely; its vast choir had a rounded apse like Norwich, but possessed the simple solemnity of the Norman style. The body of St Edmund was again verified and moved to a new shrine directly behind the high altar at the entrance to the choir, where, at long last, it was allowed to rest in peace for a hundred years.

In Jocelin of Brakelond's work there is a description of Abbot Baldwin's shrine at least as it stood a hundred years later when Abbot Samson recast it.

The high altar appears to have been under the arch dividing the choir from the transept. The shrine was directly behind it with the head of the Saint towards the altar and the feet towards the choir. From the side, the two must have appeared as though they were touching, in the shape of a capital T, with the shrine forming the upright and the altar the cross-section. In fact, however, they were separated, because the back of the altar was concave and there was a narrow passage between the two. Was it part of the pilgrimage to pass through this passage, light a candle, touch the shrine and recite appropriate prayers? Or was it purely practical to light the altar candles, get at the altar crucifix to clean it and the like? The former seems more likely because, on the shrine side of the passage was a wooden shelf or sideboard on which two candles were ever kept burning. Pilgrims probably bought candles and placed them on the shelf; the guardians would put them in due course in the candlesticks. The shelf was supported by a store-cupboard with iron doors. The presence of iron doors suggests that Baldwin had intended it to be a safe. It looks singularly like Hermann's "servatorium cum phylacteriis", the cupboard containing the relics, into which the shirt was originally placed along with St Edmund's cup and Oswen's casket with the hair and nails. At some time between 1032 and 1198, presumably after Hermann's time, say around 1100, these relics were removed. The shirt and Oswen's casket were placed over the shrine on a beam running right across the choir. The cup was put in an iron-bound box on top of the shelf right up against the shrine. This cup was certainly part of the ritual of the pilgrimage. At some time during their visit, the pilgrims drank out of it—presumably as they passed along the narrow passage behind the altar.

The relics having been removed, the cupboard was put to a very different use. It housed the dusters and polishing cloths, flax and wax, bits of unused and guttering candles: the tools and debris of a popular shrine. The cupboard abutted straight onto the base or plinth of the shrine, which was built of stone and was probably a little higher than the altar so that the shrine on top of it was visible from the nave. The reliquary of the shrine was a heavy wooden structure completely covered with plaques in repoussé silver nailed to the wood and inlaid with precious stones. There was an effigy of St Edmund in solid gold surmounting it at the altar end. Incidentally, the two candlesticks on the shelf with candles continually burning must have been of the socket variety, not spiked, because the guardians could not be bothered to clean the sockets out but stuck a new candle on top of a guttering old one: a common practice among the clergy of the twentieth century as of the tenth.

Well, on the night of Saint Etheldreda's Day, June 23rd, 1198, one of the candles at the shrine, stuck on top of a guttering one, drooped and burned the shelf. The shelf fell in on the polish, dusters, candles and rubbish in the safe below. In a trice the whole place was ablaze. Luckily it occurred in the early hours of the morning and the bellringer for Matins saw the conflagration. The fire was put out.

A pyromaniac having set fire to the candle store-cupboard in St Edmund's Church in Bury in 1969, one is in a position to know exactly how this type of fire works. It goes up with immense rapidity and generates terrific heat but does less damage than might be feared. There is no deep-seated smouldering; it is an instant surface blaze. It must have been the same in 1198. The iron doors of the cupboard were white hot; the stone of the plinth where it backed on to the cupboard crumbled at the heat; the iron-bound box containing the cup was reduced to ashes, but the cup was found intact with the cloth round it no more than scorched. Luckily, the beam with the shirt and Oswen's casket had been removed to be carved afresh. However, the shrine proper was pretty well intact: the silver plaques had not melted, neither had the gold effigy of the saint. There was a great sigh of relief. The place was cleared up as quickly as possible in the hope that the burghers would notice nothing. Of course the rumour spread round the town that the head of St Edmund had been burned up. The Abbot, the famous Abbot Samson, was absent at the time. Upon his return he reprimanded everybody all round, as was his wont.

But all things, even misfortunes, work to a good end. The fire gave Samson the opportunity to fulfil the secret ambition of his life: to verify the incorrupt body of the Martyr. In spite of the eye-witness account of Jocelin, a lot of details are not at all clear.

On the night of the Sunday after St Edmund's Day, i.e. November 22nd - 23rd, 1198, the new hood of the shrine was placed on the main altar but the body remained intact in Baldwin's shrine. This new hood was much the shape of a church without towers or transepts, a triangular roof over upright walls. It was of wood and immensely heavy, since it took six men to carry it. But a hood it was: it had no floor, like Baldwin's. One of the ends was detached so as to be able to slip the coffin under it. The inside was lined with white doe-skins. It was covered with reliefs in silver gilt. Were these the plaques of

Baldwin's shrine which had been gilt and re-assembled to fit, with a few additions? Were they new? Had Baldwin's plaques been melted down to supply the metal for them? It seems impossible to say.

After Lauds, on the morning of Monday the 23rd, the old hood was removed from Baldwin's shrine. Three layers of cloth, two of linen sandwiching one of silk, were stripped off the coffin, which lay bare. On the outside, at about neck height to St Edmund, was a relief a foot long in solid gold representing St Michael the Archangel. When did it get there? A donation of Cnut in 1032? Perhaps.

Under St Michael there was a hole in the coffin's lid where at one time the guardians used to put their hand in to verify that the body was intact. It seems probable that Ailwin was responsible for the hole. Anyway, it appears that the original lid was still there in 1198. Although woodworm had got into it before 1050, it seems that Abbot Leofstan must have halted the infestation. As has been said, the coffin was of Danish design.

The coffin was then lifted from the old shrine and carried, Jocelin lending an unbidden hand, to the high altar and was slipped under the new hood. There it remained until Wednesday evening.

During the three days, Monday morning to Wednesday evening, Baldwin's plinth was removed and Samson's put in its place. What was it like? One simply does not know. Its base may well have been of polished granite but more cannot be said. The gap between the shrine and the altar, where the cupboard and passage had been, was filled in with stone to avoid recurrence of fire.

It was confidently expected that the body would be exposed to view, as it had been so often before, on the octave of St Edmund's Day, Friday, November 27th. It was not. Samson had decided otherwise. He explained to the monks his motives for having only twelve witnesses, but, since Jocelin has not reported his speech, it is impossible to know what they were. Fear of irreverence? Fear that in the last hundred years, since the verification of 1095, the body might have fallen to dust, to the disedification of the populace? Fear that the fire had mutilated the body? Who can say?

Anyway, in the dead of night on Wednesday 25th - 26th November he performed the verification and translation of the relics. Apart from the three necessary people for a canonical verification, himself as Abbot, Hugh the Sacrist as Notary, and Walter as physician, he invited only four other distinguished monks to be present, along with his two chaplains, the two guardians of the shrine, and the two chief sacristans, making thirteen people in all including himself. Of course the greatest difficulty in a community is to keep anything secret: six other monks turned up uninvited, among whom, fortunately, was Jocelin of Brakelond. All the personnel of the sacristy was hidden up in the roof; they probably had the best view.

"So", says Jocelin, "while the monastery slept, the twelve of them, all vested in albs, drew the coffin from under the hood on the high altar and carried it to a table at the side of the shrine. They set to removing the lid, which was attached to the coffin with sixteen very long iron nails. When this was done, all were told to stand back except the two official witnesses (the notary and physician, Hugh and Walter)."

"The holy body filled the coffin completely, both lengthways and crossways, so that one could hardly put a pin between the wood and the head or feet. The head was joined to the body and was slightly raised on a pillow ..." Divers cloths were removed from the face and body until "they found the body wrapped in a linen cloth so that its outline was clearly visible."

"At this point the Abbot hesitated and said he did not dare proceed and look on the naked body of the Saint. So he took the head between his hands and said with a groan: 'O glorious Martyr, St Edmund, blessed be the day which witnessed your birth ... O glorious Martyr, do not let my daring turn to my damnation in that, a wretched sinner, I presume to touch you. You know my devotion and my intentions.' "

"He proceeded to touch the eyes and the nose, the latter very large and prominent. He then felt the chest and arms. He lifted the left hand, touched the fingers and placed his between the Saint's. Proceeding further, he came to the feet and found them upright and stiff like those of a man but lately dead. He touched the toes and counted them as he did so." ... The relic of the Cross does not appear to have been seen; presumably it was lying on St Edmund's breast beneath the cloth which wrapped the body.

It is all terribly moving. The body was covered again with the same cloths. The lid of the coffin was replaced with the same nails. Ailwin's salutations were replaced on top of the lid, beside the golden St Michael, but in the same silken pouch was placed Samson's affidavit: "In the Year of the Incarnation of the Lord One thousand One hundred and Ninety-eight, Abbot Samson, led by devotion, saw and felt the body of St Ædmund on the night following the Feast of St Catherine, in the presence of the following witnesses.'' There followed eighteen signatures: the twelve invited witnesses and the six who weren't.

A double cloth was placed on the stone plinth to absorb condensation. On top of this was a wooden plank. Over the whole was placed the great hood. The coffin, completely swathed in cloth, was slid into position. The end piece of the hood was nailed on.

That was the last time that the incorrupt body of St Edmund was beheld by mortal eye.

In the three hundred and twenty-nine years between 869 and 1198 the body had been handled by the holy woman Oswen, translated to Bury before 890, verified by Bishop Theodred in 926 or 927, viewed by the arrogant young Leofstan in the middle of the same century, washed and handled by Ailwin from 990 until the translation to London and back between 1010 and 1013, translated again at the time of Cnut's church in 1032, verified by Abbot Leofstan in 1050, re-translated to Abbot Baldwin's church in 1095, and finally verified by Abbot Samson in 1198. Few corpses can have enjoyed so public a life. Abruptly it ceases.

CHAPTER SEVEN

From Bury to Toulouse

What happened? What became of this famous relic? Perhaps it stayed on in Samson's shrine until it was destroyed at the Dissolution in 1539, without ever being translated or verified again. So the body constantly examined in the 329 years between 869 and 1198 was not examined once in the 341 years from 1198 to 1539? It is, of course, possible but, on the face of it seems hardly likely.

Is there any other explanation? There is, and, in view of the extraordinary lack of evidence for the presence of the body in Bury, it is worth examining. It is that the body was stolen by Lewis the Dolphin (later Lewis VIII, King of France) and found its way to the Basilica of St Sernin at Toulouse.

But how could relics among the most famous in England be whisked away without anybody noticing it? It sounds highly improbable. Is it even possible?

Possible it certainly is. Four months after Samson had verified the relics, on April 6th ,1199, Richard I died. The Abbot had always been a staunch supporter of Richard, which meant automatically that he was no favourite with his brother, John. Much has been done in recent years to whitewash King John. Even if it is all true, the fact remains that he had a strange sense of humour and an uncanny knack of making himself unpopular. Immediately after his coronation he came to Bury. He and his court enjoyed the hospitality of the Abbey. It was presumed that he would make some princely gift in return. One of his servants borrowed a length of silk from the Sacristan. With much pomp and ceremony the King presented it to the Abbey. He never even paid for it. It is, of course, frightfully funny. John must have had a hearty laugh. But people do not like being laughed at; it is not the best way to make friends. John certainly had none in Bury.

In March 1208, the Pope laid England under an Interdict. In October 1209 he excommunicated John. During this difficult period Samson managed the affairs of the Abbey as, perhaps, nobody else could have done. He obtained from John that St Edmund's Abbey be excluded from the general confiscation of ecclesiastical revenue which

John imposed in retaliation for the Interdict. But Samson died on December 30th, 1212. The King was still excommunicated—until his surrender to the Holy See on May 15th, 1213.

To elect an Abbot when one's country is under an Interdict and one's king excommunicated presents unusual problems. However, the monks succeeded in imposing their candidate, Hugh de Northwold. As far as the present study is concerned, he was clearly elected on an anti-John ticket. His very election illustrates the feeling of the monks. It is not in the least surprising that Hugh allowed the conjuration of the barons which led to the signing of Magna Carta to take place in Bury in 1214, although he was careful himself to be absent.

Concerning Abbot Hugh he was considered to be the "flower of the black monks", an exemplary Benedictine. In politics he followed the lead of the Holy See. Anti-John by temperament, he nonetheless veered towards him after the lifting of excommunication, which explains his absence from the conjuration of the barons in 1214. The following year he went so far as to receive his temporalities from the King. After John's death in October, 1216, Hugh certainly sided with the Legate, Cardinal Guala, and William the Marshall in support of John's son, Henry III.

It would be very foolish, however, to imagine that every monk in the Abbey followed the Abbot's political changes. A hard core of "baronial" monks must have survived. To them the rightful king of England was not John or his child but Lewis the Dolphin. It is true that the Holy See had always avoided underwriting Lewis' claim during John's excommunication, but it is equally true that a fair section of the baronage and the burghers of those towns most in contact with the Continent, London and the south and east coasts, all accepted him. It is probably not unfair to say that had John lived a little longer Lewis would have become generally recognised as king of England.

John died in the nick of time. On behalf of the papacy the Legate, Guala, promptly recognised the boy King Henry III and excommunicated Lewis for attacking a feudatory of the Holy See—for such, in medieval terms, the kingdom of England had become since John's surrender to the Papacy in 1213.

Although it was more difficult to appear as an heroic liberator against an innocent boy than against his discredited father, Lewis's cause was by no means desperate in the middle of 1217. It was severely shaken, but no more, on May 12th by his principal ally, the Earl of Winchester, losing the Battle of Lincoln. The remnants of the Earl's army made its way back to London and safety by the direct southern road. Half-way between Sleaford and Bourne they passed Sempringham.

St Gilbert of Sempringham was the popular saint of the day. He was the only English founder of a monastic order, the Gilbertines. He had died aged 100 and more in 1189. He had been canonised by Innocent III within the century, in 1201. It seems more than likely that it was the Earl of Winchester who stole his relics while the going was good and presented them to Lewis upon his arrival in London. The gain of a Saint might compensate for the loss of a battle.

The loss of the Battle of Lincoln was more important psychologically than militarily. As Powick so rightly observes, after the battle Lewis's English chivalry "flocked to change sides". It was vital to get hold of more cavalry, more knights. Lewis wrote to his wonderful wife, Blanche of Castille, in whose name incidentally he claimed the crown of England since she was the granddaughter of Henry II, to recruit for him in Flanders. It was early in July 1217 that the Lady Blanche arrived at Calais to open her knightly recruiting office. As in everything else she undertook, she was completely successful.

In the meantime, her husband had to keep the remnants of his chivalry reasonably but safely occupied and preferably out of London. This explains the expedition to Bury.

It is singularly unfortunate that in his monumental study on the life and reign of Lewis VIII (1894) Petit-Dutaillis should have stated categorically that Lewis spared all monastic property except Westminster and Canterbury, adding "The authors of the Monasticon Anglicanum claim that Lewis also plundered the monastry of St Edmund and brought back to France the body of the Saint. There is not a word about it in contemporary narratives." It is an extraordinary lapse of memory on the part of so distinguished an historian but the statement is quite untrue. As M. Bordier has pointed out, the contemporary and often eye-witness author of the "History of the Dukes of Normandy" (edited by F. Michel, Paris, 1840) reports the following: "Puis envoya Looys le visconte de Meleun o grand chevalerie vers St Edmond, pour tenser la terre. En cele voie ala Wistasses de Noeville, qui en toutes les besoignes voloit aler, et Hughes Tracons et plusiour autre. Chil fisent lor chevauchie, si barroiierent la ville de St Edmond et gaagnerent mmoult proie par la terre, et puis s'en repairierent a Londres. En cel point que cele chevauchie dut mouvoir, estoit me dame Blanche, la femme de Looys, a Kalais, u elle assambloit toutes les gens et les chevaliers qu'ele pooit avoir, por envoier en Engletierre son segnour secourre."

There can be no doubt about it: in July 1217, while the Lady Blanche was at Calais, Lewis sent an important detachment of cavalry to Bury under the command of the Viscount of Melun. That Bury was not in fact sacked only shows that the expedition must have got what it wanted without such violence. This is certainly the point in history when the body of St Edmund could have been stolen. It is also the point when the Toulouse tradition says it was.

It is true that the body cannot have been given to Melun by the Abbot. Not only would such an act be clean contrary to the known character of Abbot Hugh as well as to his interests, but, as has already been said, by this time he was wholeheartedly behind the Legate and the Marshall—which explains his later promotion to the See of Ely.

It must therefore have been a theft. But a theft implies the connivance of some half-dozen monks, of whom one at least held office—sub-prior, sacrist, guardian or the like. Could such be found? It would require a very superficial acquaintance of England in 1217 to say that they could not.

Perhaps it is worthwhile at this point to consider the possibility of substitution, not unknown in the history of relics; that the monks palmed off a false body on the viscount and kept the real one. Had there been a sack of the borough, substitution might well have been attempted; but there was none. What was given appears to have been given willingly: there was no point in giving a fake. Moreover, had a fake been given, after Lewis' departure from England two months later, there would have been cries of exaltation in Bury, probably with exposition of the body to prove how the clever monks had outwitted the silly soldiers. There was none. Lastly, whereas substitution might be easy with bones, it would be impossible with an incorrupt body. Even if the monks happened to have a corpse to hand, the viscount cannot be presumed to have been such a fool as to accept a fresh body for one dessicated and incorrupt, now 350 years old.

It must also be remembered that there was no great physical difficulty in removing the coffin from the shrine. Jocelin's description has been excellently summed up by J. R. Thomson (Records of St Edmund, 1890, p. 143): "the shrine (feretrem, i.e. reliquary) was a removable cover of great weight, and open at the bottom and fitted over the coffin (loculus); the latter lay on a marble basis but separated from it by cloths and a board or tray to protect it from moisture. All these particulars should be borne in mind when considering the removal of St Edmund's body from Bury.'' Why should they be considered? Because it is perfectly clear that all that was needed was a couple of crowbars to lever up the end of the cover or hood and slip the coffin out. It could be done in a trice, silently and without a gang of workmen.

So, it is claimed, the body of St Edmund journeyed up to London for the second time. It must have been a very different trip from that of 1010 when the monk Ailwin lovingly pushed the litter. The Viscount of Melun, Eustace de Neville and Hugh Tracons were highly unlikely to display the same solicitude. It would not be in the least surprising if the incorrupt body was shaken to dust in the course of the cavalcade. It will never be seen incorrupt again.

A month after the body's arrival in London, on August 24th, the Lady Blanche despatched her knights from Calais to reinforce her husband, under the leadership of Eustace the Monk. On the following day at the Battle for Sandwich, Eustace was completely defeated and was beheaded in the hold of his own ship. Along with his boats, Lewis' cause was sunk. On September 12th he signed the Treaty of Kingston with the Legate and the Marshall. For the huge sum of 10,000 marks and an amnesty for his followers, he surrendered London and returned to France with all his bag and baggage, which included, of course, the remains of St Edmund and St Gilbert. In those days princes collected relics as today boys do postage stamps.

Upon his return to France Lewis was immediately despatched by his father, Philip Augustus, to prosecute the crusade against the Albigenses. In all probability this was the most hypocritical exhibition of charlatanry in the Middle Ages, but its history lies outside the scope of the present study. Anyway, Lewis still with bag and baggage, with St Edmund and St Gilbert, found himself besieging Toulouse.

The history of the siege remains surprisingly obscure in spite of the wealth of contemporary documents. It should be remembered that, even at this late date, Toulouse was much more of a capital city than was Paris. It still looked that it would be the centre of a great Mediterranean kingdom including Aragon, Barcelona, Languedoc and Provence. In 1218-19 Toulouse was divided into two distinct sections: the City and the Borough. The City lay to the east and included the Roman city, the cathedral, the capitol and the rest; the Borough lay to the west and was not much built up in 1218, although it included the great Abbey of Saint Sernin on its western side, almost against the City. The whole was walled. By 1218 the internal wall which had separated the City from the Borough had been demolished, but there was still an earthwork and a continuous line of houses which had once backed on to it.

Lewis approached from the west. He seems to have captured the Borough, since there are letters of his dated from St Sernin, but he failed to penetrate the City. The great fortress of the Counts of Toulouse was right on the other side, on the eastern extremity of the City. It becomes fairly obvious that if Lewis failed to carry the City he was in dire danger of himself being besieged in the Borough. If the line of the City held, then Raymond VII could emerge from the fortress and besiege the Borough from the west. Lewis would be cut off and captured. He fled abruptly leaving bag and baggage, including of course St Edmund and St Gilbert. So ended the siege of 1219.

Basing himself on Mgr de Montchal's admirable ''Mandement'' of 1644, M. Bordier says that Lewis gave the relics to St Sernin, but this is not so. Obviously, writing at the start of the ''Grand Siècle'', Montchal was not going to remind the new little King, Lewis XIV, that the relics he was extolling had been captured by the Toulousians from the King's direct ancestor. This correction is not unimportant because the greatest difficulty in the Toulouse story was why Lewis should go to considerable trouble to steal relics in England in order to give them to Raymond VII of Toulouse. It does not make sense, especially as Toulouse only became part of the royal domain of France on the death of Raymond's daughter, Jeanne, on August 22nd, 1271. But the problem is solved; Lewis never gave the relics at all: they were captured.

E. E. Swain, Hunstanton.

(ix) Known as St Edmund's Point, Hunstanton, Norfolk, it was near here that Edmund landed when he arrived in East Anglia.

E. E. Swain, Hunstanton.

(x) Remains of Chapel believed to be on the site where King Edmund built his Royal Palace at Hunstanton.

Walter Blythin, Clacton-on-Sea.

(xvi) The exterior of Greenstead Church showing the timber wall construction.

John Seymour, Norwich.

(xviii) Norwich Cathedral built out of the 4d a carucate granted by Cnut to St Edmund.

CHAPTER EIGHT

The Toulouse Evidence

It is one thing to show that the relics could have been stolen in 1217 and left at St Sernin two years later, and quite another to show that they were. What is the Toulouse evidence prior to the dissolution of the Abbey at Bury in 1539? It is late in date but by no means negligible.

Saint Sernin, consecrated by Urban II, must bid fair to being the greatest monument of the 11th century in Christendom. It was an Abbey of Augustinian Canons. Apart from being on the road to Compostella, it was a place of pilgrimage in its own right. It had a quite incredible collection of relics. These were and still are housed in three separate groups. First comes the "armoires" or cupboards. These are built into the walls of the deambulatory behind the choir and the five radial chapels which give off from it. Then there is the small upper crypt directly under the high altar, which contained the relics from the "martyrium" of the original Roman church—notably St Saturninus the Martyr (St Sernin), first Bishop of Toulouse. Then a lower crypt, choirwards from the high altar.

The upper crypt is clearly contemporary with the basilica and must have been built shortly before 1090. The vault of the lower crypt is, curiously enough, much later; it is in "primitive gothic" and must date from about 1220. The walls of the lower crypt, however, appear far more ancient; they may well be part of the eighth century Carolingian basilica. In fact, it looks as though it was decided in about 1220 to enlarge the crypt—perhaps because new relics had arrived—and in doing so the builders fell through as it were, to the Carolingian ground level. It is certain, from the Mandement of 1644 that the relics of St Edmund and St Gilbert were placed in the lower crypt. Incidentally, a visit to this lower crypt did not form part of the pilgrimage to Saint Sernin. This consisted in reciting the appropriate prayers at each of the cupboards of the deambulatory and touching the tomb of St Saturninus in the upper crypt.

The old relics at St Sernin, that is those which were there prior to 1500, fall into four perfectly clear categories. First come the local saints from the Roman period, St Saturninus, St Papulus, and the like.

Then there are the gifts of Charlemagne, who before the disaster of Roncesvalles in 778, had intended Toulouse to be the south-western capital of the Empire: notably the fragments of the Apostles and the Roman Martyrs Claudius, Nicostrates and the rest. Thirdly there are the incredible pious bibolets sent back by Raymond IV from the first Crusade, such as Saint Suzannah of Babylon. Alas! far the most imaginative of Raymond's relics—the stone with which St Stephen was lapidated—has been withdrawn from public veneration in this unpoetic age. The fourth group sticks out like a sore thumb amidst such splendours: St Edmund and St Gilbert. Their sheer incongruity is highly suggestive.

There is another relic in the lower crypt which is thought-provoking: a fragment of the True Cross. Artistically the most beautiful object in the crypt is a reliquary for the Cross in Limoges enamel of the mid-thirteenth century, depicting how a lawyer of Toulouse, one Maître Bourdadel, obtained the relic. But curiously enough, the archives of St Sernin show no connection between the reliquary and the relic. The reference in the authoritative monograph on St Sernin by Rey and Auriol is certainly mistaken. Neither was the relic among those of Charlemagne or of Raymond IV. Traditionally it was given to St Sernin by Alfonso of Poitiers, son of our Lewis and husband of Jeanne of Toulouse, daughter of Raymond VII. It seems just possible that Lewis, when he decamped, took the relic from among St Edmund's bones and gave it to Alfonso who was induced to restore it by his wife. It seems more likely however that it was simply found along with the bones of St Edmund. Incidentally, it is not being suggested that the presence of the Cross authenticates the presence of St Edmund. It is rather the other way round: the presence of St Edmund provides the likely source for the relic of the Cross.

To return to St Edmund, proof of the antiquity and unanimity of the Toulouse tradition lies in the fact of his being one of the eight protectors of the City. When this came about no one knows, but probably in the early part of the fourteenth century when patrons and protectors became fashionable. That it came about no one can doubt. There, painted on the vast hexagonal columns on either side of the choir of St Sernin stand the protectors. On the gospel side Saints Saturninus, Papulus, George and Julitta with the little Cyrus; on the epistle side Saints Suzannah of Babylon, Honoratus, Hilarius, and "S. EADMUNDUS REX ANGLIAE". The existing paintings are datable to about 1575, to the start of the reign of Henry III, but, as is well known, such decorations are invariably overlaid on older representations of identical subjects. Besides, in the middle of the Wars of Religion, nobody is going to invent on the quiet a new protector for the town and a bogus one at that.

The most extraordinary thing about the fresco is the Anglo-Saxon spelling of "Eadmundus". It is very difficult to see how this can have got there if the Canons of St Sernin were not in possession of the body. The fact is that the Anglo-Saxon "Ea", pronounced as an elongated "Ay", not as the short "E" in the modern Edmund, disappears from current usage at the end of the twelfth century. Even Jocelin of Brakelond gives Abbot Samson's text of verification as "Corpus sancti Ædmundi" with the reversed Anglo-Norman or Latin diphthong. It is true that in the Bury Chronicle (edited by Antonia Gransden), although Edmund predominates from 1212 to 1267, after that date Eadmund recurs, but it is a self-conscious touch of antiquarianism and East-Anglian Englishry which could not have affected the spelling at Toulouse. It is noteworthy that in the beautiful thirteenth century calendar of the Jacobins preserved in the Municipal Library at Toulouse, Edward the Confessor appears as "Eduardus" and not as "Eaduardus". More important still, the history of the Dukes of Normandy, written in 1219 and already quoted, gives the name as "Edmond".

The only way the Canons of St Sernin were likely to get hold of the correct spelling was from the possession of the corpse. With it, as has already been seen, were two documents: the verification of Abbot Samson and the salutations of the monk Ailwin. Although Jocelin gives Samson's text as "Corpus sancti Ædmundi" it may be doubted if it really was. Samson was an East-Anglian and commonly preached in the local dialect. He would be likely to write Eadmund quite automatically. Equally automatically Jocelin would correct his master's barbarism. However that may be, the salutations of Ailwin were written in Anglo-Saxon and would certainly give the spelling Eadmund. It looks very much as though St Sernin must have had the relics, as it certainly appears to have had the connected documents.

Alas, the stone sarcophagus in which the relics rested until 1644 has disappeared. There is a description of it in the Acts of Verification carried out on July 16th of that year. On the front of it "in large black lettering" (in the singular: "en grosse lettre noire") was: "Icy repose le venerable corps de Sainct Edmond Martyr Roy d'Angleterre." Fairly certainly, of course, nothing of the sort was written on it but an equivalent latin text. How the Edmund was spelt we have no means of knowing. All that is certain is that the text was easily recognisable as referring to an Edmund, King of England. The sarcophagus was still in existence in 1853 but no exact transcription was taken. According to d'Aldeguier, the distinguished local historian, it was built into the wall behind the altar of the chapel in which it lay. Maybe, but according to a note of one of the curates at St Sernin preserved in the archives, it appears to have been broken up as rubble. At all events, the vast marble sarcophagus at present in the chapel of St Edmund at St Sernin is not it. If only it had been preserved one might have learned a lot from "the large black lettering". Unfortunately, there is always a vandal around the corner. Ignorance destroys more than premeditation. We have seen it in our own time, when the most glorious cultural heritage of the world, the Roman Missal, has been jettisoned by Pope, Bishop, and priest with the fatuous flippancy of fools.

The documentary evidence at Toulouse is late in date, for the very simple reason that nothing earlier has survived. Earlier lists of the relics in the cupboards of the deambulatory are not lacking, but the first complete list of relics to have come down to us is that made by Canons Jean David and Dominique de Peyron, along with the notary, Etienne Telhet. They held two sessions, the first on August 11th, the second on December 12th, 1489. Entry 291 of the Second Session reads: "Item ... Et sancti Aymondi, regis Anglie quondam ... in superiori vase corpus dicti beati Aymondi." That is: "Item ... of St Aymond, once a King of England ... the body of the said Blessed Aymond in the top container."

A second inventory was made on May 6th, 1504. Entry No. 22 reads: "Item, fuit reperta una magna capsa lapidea super unum altare, ubi fertur corpus sancti Aymundi quondam regis Anglie quiescere." "A large stone casket was found over an altar where the body of St Aymund is said to rest." The word "fertur" is a little ambiguous. It could mean "it is said"—in the abstract—although "ubi ferunt quiescere", or "ubi, ut fertur, quiescit" would be more natural. It is more likely to mean "where is stated to rest the body of St Aymund", referring to the text in great black lettering which was found on the sarcophagus in 1644. Both the above lists are now in the Archives of the Département of the Haute Garonne. There is a third list, drawn up in 1534, in the archives of St Sernin. This is a "Vidimus", that is a notarially certified copy, of the first list of 1489. The fact is that, prior to the Dissolution at Bury, in three official inventories, including the earliest to survive, Toulouse has claimed the relics of St Edmund.

There are also unofficial documents of the same period. The Municipal Library at Toulouse (C.75) has a breviary of the Diocese of Rodez dated 1443; it has a list of relics at St Sernin on its fly-leaf. Column 2, lines 4 and 5 read: "Item, corpus bti Aymundi cfs et Regis Anglie." The list is obviously later than the breviary but how much later it is difficult to say. The historical Commission of 1902 dates it as "from the middle of the fifteenth century". It is in very small and beautiful handwriting, but probably difficult to place much before 1470. The interest of the text lies in its inserting "Cfs"—Confessor—after the name, and inserting an "et" between "Cfs" and "Regis Anglie", just in case somebody should be so foolish as to misconstrue the latin as "Confessor of a King of England".
No precaution, however, is ever adequate. As will be seen, this is precisely what happened.

The next unofficial document is clearly dependent on the former, so much so that it looks as though the one is the manuscript notes for the other. In 1515 Maître Nicolas Bertrand, of a distinguished legal family at Toulouse, published a beautiful incunabulum called the "Gesta Tholosanorum". It contains a list of major relics at St Sernin. Folio V, line V, reads: "Item, corpus beati Aymundi Confessoris Regis Anglie". This perfectly simple text, "the body of Blessed Aymund, confessor, King of England," acquires as unexpected as ill-deserved a history. In 1517 a certain Antoine Leblanc published an anonymous translation of Maître Bertrand's work. It ran through several editions up to 1555, at least two of which were prior to the Dissolution at Bury. In his preface the translator writes that "at the risk of his small and humble understanding" he had undertaken the translation "in favour of common folk who did not understand the complications of Latin." Unfortunately neither did the translator. Me. Bertrand's text becomes precisely "Le corps du bienheureux Aymond, Confesseur du Roi d'Angleterre"—"Aymond, Confessor to the King of England"! Incredible, but so it is. In the controversy of 1901, which will be dealt with in due course, Sir Ernest Clarke pounced on this schoolboy howler with a shriek of joy: there! Toulouse had never really claimed to possess the body of St Edmund at all but merely that of a holy confessor of an unnamed English King!

Naturally enough Sir Ernest also found it impossible to identify the "Aymund" of Toulouse with our Edmund. This is rubbish. If anything, the Toulouse spelling proves its great antiquity. The "Ay" is an attempt to indicate the long sound of the Anglo-Saxon "Ea", which could scarcely have been known to them had the body arrived later than the thirteenth century. Moreover, the "Aymund" or "Aymond" of the list is the same person as the S. Eadmundus on the choir column. Conversely, the Eadmundus of the column has been in Toulouse long enough to have acquired a local appellation, "Aymond", both in official and unofficial documents.

M. Bordier has unearthed evidence that the canons of St Sernin knew exactly to whom the relics belonged and knew it "from time immemorial" (Pages 108-9). In 1644, prior to the elevation and procession of the relics, Archbishop de Montchal wished to proceed with their canonical verification. One of the Canons opposed this on the ground that the Abbey was exempt from episcopal jurisdiction and because the relics were already verified by immemorial custom. In support of the latter argument this is what he wrote: "The oldest breviaries, missals, calendars of the said Church (St Sernin) testify to the feast which is celebrated on account of the said relic (St Edmund) on November 20th in the said church ... (two illegible words) that there is no evidence to the contrary". ("Les plus vieux breviaires, missels, calendriers de la dite église marquent la fête qui se célèbre à raison de la dite relique le 20 novembre dans la dite Eglise depuis ... qu'il n'est mémoire du contraire"). The Canons certainly knew who their "Aymund" was, since they knew his feast fell on November 20th.

The tragedy is that not a single breviary, missal or calendar of St Sernin has survived from before the seventeenth century. The Municipal Library has splendid medieval examples from every other religious house in the City, notably the Dominicans and Austin Friars, but from St Sernin, nothing. Presumably what had not been dispersed by commendatory Abbots in the eighteenth century was destroyed at the Revolution. However, it would be very unrealistic to suppose that the Canon of St Sernin in question had no medieval evidence to hand in support of his argument against the Bishop.

One last word about the Toulouse evidence before returning to Bury. The unofficial documents, the Rodez Breviary and Me. Bertrand, both refer to St Edmund as "Confessor". This presents no particular difficulty, as the clear-cut distinction between "Confessor", as one who confessed by heroic practice of the virtues, and "Martyr", as one who confessed by shedding his blood, is of comparatively modern origin. Indeed, as for St Edmund, Me. Bertrand uses the term "confessor" for St Honestus, whom he certainly knew to be a martyr as he appears in the martyrologies under February 16th. What the use of the term probably implies is that Me. Bertrand must have acquired his information from a source considerably earlier than the fifteenth century, by which time the two terms had indeed become distinct.

The Toulouse evidence prior to the Dissolution at Bury in 1539 has been examined in some detail because it has not been readily available in England. It is by no means negligible. There is a corpse. It has been identified with the correct Anglo-Saxon spelling. His Feast is celebrated on the correct day, November 20th, and that since "time immemorial" by 1644. He has been there long enough to have acquired a local appellation, Aymund, itself a suggestive attempt at the correct pronunciation. He appears in the earliest extant list of the complete collection of relics. Although all the Toulouse evidence points to a very much earlier presence, on subsisting documents alone St Sernin was claiming to possess the relics of St Edmund for over half a century before the Dissolution at Bury. The monks at Bury did nothing to undeceive them.

CHAPTER NINE

Bury until the Dissolution

It is time to return to Bury. As has been seen, in July, 1217, the body must have been stolen without the knowledge of Abbot Hugh de Northwold. A handful of monks, including an officer of the Abbey, would be implicated, but that would be all. They had handed over the body of the patron of England to Lewis whom they regarded as their lawful King. Doubtless it would be brought back with great rejoicing once the King had come into his own, thanks to the heavenly intercession of St Edmund. As we know, things turned out differently. In less than two months Lewis had signed the Treaty of Kingston and sailed for France without ever again setting foot in England.

Lewis, of course, could not return the relics to Bury, even had he wanted to, without involving the monks who had helped to steal them. One of Lewis' many good qualities was his loyalty to his inferiors. On the other hand, the monks of Bury were supremely unlikely to divulge the theft. Their secret must have died with them as it was against their own interest to reveal it. The last of them was doubtless dead before 1250.

The routine at the empty shrine continued uninterrupted.

How long could this state of affairs go on without news of the Toulouse claim percolating back to Bury? None can say. It had presumably not got back by 1257 because a Bury Charter of that year bears the phrase in reference to St Edmund "Cujus corpus requiesciet ibidem"—"whose body rests in the said place."

Perhaps however one can risk a fairly intelligent guess. In the first place, it should be remembered that Lewis was very unlikely to talk much about his relics, not merely to protect his supporters in Bury but because he can scarcely have been proud of having to leave them in Toulouse. As for the Canons of St Sernin, they doubtless swooped down with great joy on the relics in 1219: Saints Edmund and Gilbert were a welcome addition to their amazing collection. But the rejoicing was probably short lived. Prudence is a virtue not to be despised. There were ecclesiastical censures against the stealing of relics; these could perhaps be discounted, as the Canons had certainly not stolen them themselves. Worse, the English might claim them back; pressure could be brought on Raymond VII since his mother was a sister of King John of England. Worse still, Lewis might claim them, especially after he had become Lewis VIII, King of France, in 1223. Prudence! Prudence!

Fifty years is not a long time in a great Abbey; it is enormous in political history. In August, 1272, Jeanne of Toulouse died and the territory passed to the royal domain of France. Lewis VIII was dead, so was his son, Lewis IX; a grandson, Philip III was reigning. In England, Henry III, in whose minority the relics had been stolen, was buried in Westminster Abbey on St Edmund's Day, November 20th, of the same year. Anyway, fifty years of unmolested possession gave the canons a prescriptive right to the relics under canon law. No longer was there cause for prudence.

Of course, it could be no more than a coincidence that shortly afterwards a sudden interest was taken in St Edmund's relics in Bury. It is quite certain that in 1275 the litter in which St Edmund had been brought back to Bury by the monk Ailwin in 1013 was removed from "the old chapel of St Edmund" (i.e. not the shrine), at the angle formed by the north-transept and the choir, and was placed in the chapel of St Stephen. The old chapel was totally demolished and the site excavated. The new Lady Chapel was erected in its place.

But that is unlikely to be all that happened. Already in 1886 Lord Francis Hervey had pointed out that the shrine illustrated in Lydgate's beautiful fifteenth century manuscript, presented to Henry VI and now in the British Museum, showed the shrine of St Edmund at that time to be considerably later in date than Abbot Samson. It is true that there are a dozen quite different drawings of the shrine in the manuscript, all imaginary and generic, in the best unrepresentational manner of the period; but the larger, coloured version of Henry VI praying at the shrine is likely, as Mackinlay pointed out, to be representational. In this version, the base is painted red and probably represents granite from Samson's shrine, but the main under-structure above it, is painted green; this almost certainly represents the presence of Purbeck marble. The tracery is of the early Decorated Period and could date from any time between 1270 and 1320. One cannot help feeling that the construction of the new shrine for the body (or at least the embellishment of the old) would go hand in hand with the rehousing of the minor relic (the litter) and the building of the Lady Chapel. The extraordinary thing is that with all this activity going on there was no verification of the continued presence of the incorrupt body. By now it was nearly eighty years since anyone had seen it.

A possible explanation for the activity around the relics and the absence of any verification would be that somewhere around 1272 - 74 news of the Toulouse claim reached Bury. The Abbot, Simon de Luton, felt he could easily disprove it by the obvious means of conducting a verification of the body. In preparation for so great an event, the lower part of the shrine was remodelled. To remodel the upper part, however, it would be advisable to remove the hood and place the body on the high altar, as Abbot Samson had done. This, of course, would be prior to the verification. However, the hood didn't have to be lifted more than a couple of inches or its end removed, when it would become clear that there was no coffin beneath it. So disastrous a discovery would not for a moment convince the Abbot of the truth of the Toulouse claim. Of course, St Edmund was at Bury! If the body was not in the shrine, then it had been hidden elsewhere for greater safety. This, incidentally, was not an uncommon practice, as may be seen from the case of St Francis of Assisi. But the relics must have been hidden a long time previously because he, Simon, had been Abbot since 1257, all through the Barons' War.

Nobody seemed to know where the relics were. A diligent search produced no results. The most likely place was somewhere in St Edmund's Chapel. The Chapel was accordingly demolished and the site excavated. It was part of the operation "hunt the body". Body they found none. What they did find was the foundations of Cnut's Church, consecrated in 1032. This interpretation of the events around 1275 would explain why no verification or exposition of a supposedly incorrupt body was ever attempted right up to the Dissolution in 1539, a period of over two and a half centuries. It was known at Bury that the shrine was empty.

Incidentally it is precisely at this period that St George begins to supplant St Edmund as patron of England. Even though Richard I may have adopted St George as a personal patron, the first appearance of his arms in any official connection is on a seal of Lyme Regis of 1284 which shows a warship flying the white ensign, the red St George's cross on a white background. It is only between 1345 and 1349, however, the period of the foundation of the Order of the Garter and of the Battle of Crecy, that St George really ousts St Edmund. It is not impossible that the change is connected with the knowledge in court circles of the presence of the latter's relics in Toulouse. But Edmund died slowly. Perhaps his last appearance is his most famous. On the wonderful Wilton Diptych in the National Gallery, Richard II (1377-99) is shown with St John the Baptist, his personal patron, with St Edward the Confessor, patron of the royal family, and with St Edmund, patron of the country. But then, Richard II was very old-fashioned and nostalgic of the past.

Of course the disappearance of the relics altered nothing at Bury. It remained the shrine of the patron of England. Even if the body could not be found, his belongings were still there, his hair and nail parings, his shirt and cup and litter. Moreover, even the most superstitious medieval monk did not imagine for a second that one had to possess a piece of bone in order to adore God in his saints! So as not to upset the piety of the faithful and incur the wrath of the citizens, the fact of the disappearance of the body would not be publicized and everything at the shrine would go on as usual. Even if the Canons at St Sernin, by some means totally unknown at Bury, had got hold of the body, they were not to be allowed "to get away with it". Does anybody really expect Abbot Simon to admit that the Abbey had failed in its trust as guardian of St Edmund and to issue a canonical authentication in favour of the relics at Toulouse? This is nonsense. On the other hand there is no question of the monks at Bury being morally guilty of encouraging devotion at an empty shrine, as was said in the polemics of 1901. What happened was that devotion at the shrine continued, whether the relics were there or not, just as today there are pilgrimages to Walsingham although the Holy House has long since vanished. The fact is that pious people are not as superstitious as agnostics feel they should be.

It is the fact that the routine at Bury continued unchanged which explains the only evidence of the presence of the body in the Abbey. This is the "aggregations". Pious laymen and benefactors were "aggregated" to the spiritual benefit of the Abbey. Like the freeman of a modern borough, a scroll was issued to the person so honoured. The form, the wording, of these aggregations is known from the Paston aggregation in 1429. The text bears: "for the devotion which you have to God and our monastery, in which the glorious king and martyr, St Edmund, corporally and incorruptly resteth ... ".

As a matter of fact this evidence is not as solid as its supporters have made out. The hallowed phrase "cujus corpus incorruptum ... ", "whose incorrupt body resteth", does not appear in any surviving document between the Charter of 1257 already mentioned, and the Aggregation of the Duke of Lancaster in 1392. After that date aggregations seem to have become fairly common. Hervey mentions one in 1415. There is the Paston one in 1429 and a whole group of them around the visit of Henry VI in 1433. Lydgate's poem of the same date also refers to the corporal presence of the Saint. After Abbot Curteys's death in 1446, however, aggregations, and with them the hallowed phrase, seem to disappear.

The hallowed phrase cannot be taken as good evidence of the presence of the body precisely because a hallowed phrase it is. To leave it out on public documents would be tantamount to publicising the absence of the body. Moreover, as has already been said, the mere fact that the monks could not produce the body does not mean that they believed it was not there but in Toulouse. There is in fact one tiny shred of evidence that the body was thought to be buried on the premises. It occurs in the Register known as Curteys I. (B.M. add 14 848). It gives an unexpected twist to the hallowed phrase: "cum monasterium gloriosi regis et martyris Sti Edmundi in quo incorruptum ipsius corpus requiescit humatum ... "—"the monastery in which the incorrupt body lies *buried*." In latin the word "humatum", interred, sticks out very conspicuously. Only in one other instance is it used in connection with St Edmund's relics, by Abbo, when the body was "humatum" in the neighbourhood of Hellesdon before there ever was a shrine. Even in general it is not a word one would use of a body in a shrine but, placed as it is, an unnecessary addition to the hallowed phrase, it becomes highly significant. In its context it can only imply that the author thought the incorrupt body was buried somewhere on the premises, because he knew the shrine was empty.

At Bury the routine continued unchanged. No new Oswen trimmed the Saint's beard. No monk Ailwin washed his face. No Ælfgeth complained that spiders were spinning their webs over his face or the woodworm sprinkling dust on his body. No one thought he might be given new clothes. They just issued aggregations, "where the incorrupt body resteth", but nobody thought of looking to see if incorrupt it still was. Two hundred and sixty-seven years passed.

In 1465 came the Great Fire. Dr Montague James discovered and published in his history (pp. 204 - 212) an eye-witness account. The fire broke out because of the carelessness of some workmen repairing the lead of the roof. It was terrific. The central tower collapsed; the debris must have piled up within a few feet of the shrine, the other side of the High Altar. The flames spread along the choir roof. The tester over St Edmund caught fire, crashed onto the shrine, broke in two and lay burning merrily on either side of it. Two heroic laymen broke in through a window and started coping with the flames.

Eventually the fire was extinguished. Miracle! The shrine was intact: "indempni feretro"! Incidentally, the cross-beam with Oswen's casket and the shirt escaped: the roof above and tester below were in flames but not it. This really does seem miraculous.

It will be remembered that the fairly insignificant fire of the reliquary cupboard furnished the excuse for Abbot Samson to verify the body in 1198, the last time it had been seen in Bury. This vast conflagration will obviously make Abbot Bohun proceed to a similar verification? Oh no it won't! The tower was rebuilt, the roof repaired, the building restored and the shrine untouched! Had the Abbot believed that the relics were there he would have been in conscience bound to verify their condition. After all, it was an incorrupt body that was supposed to be present. Incidentally, Sir Ernest Clarke, who agreed that the relics were not there at the Dissolution in 1539 (which will be dealt with shortly) believed they had been reduced to ashes in the fire. This will not work. The shrine was reasonably intact, "indempni feretro". Now, the temperature at which bones pulverize is immeasurably greater than that at which a structure of old, dry wood, covered with plaques of silver-gilt, would disintegrate and melt. Had the relics been in the shrine the bones at least would have survived. The only plausible explanation for the extraordinary event of there being no verification of the body is that there were no relics there and Abbot Bohun knew it.

The history of the Reformation and Dissolution of the major Abbeys is outside the scope of the present study. Suffice it to say that the Dissolution was carried out with scrupulous care and the utmost ruthlessness. The best eye-witness account is probably that of Chauncey on the suppression of the London Charterhouse. Inventories of all relics, church plate and valuables were in the hands of the Commissioners. At Bury they had been checked and brought up-to-date in the summer of 1535.

Concerning shrines and relics, the instructions to the Commissioners have survived in the case of St Richard of Chichester: they were to "remove the shrine and bones with all the ornaments of the said shrine belonging" and to see that "both the shrine and the place where it was kept be destroyed even to the ground". The same would be done at Bury. So at last, even if it be under most tragic circumstances, there must be a final verification of the incorrupt body of St Edmund.

There was not. No eye-witness account of the sacrilege exists, but there are two letters from the Commissioners to Thomas Cromwell.

The first is dated November 5th, 1539, the day of the surrender of the Abbey: "......Amongst the reliques we founde moche vanitie and superstition, as the coles that St Laurence was tosted withal, the paring of St Edmundes naylles, S Thomas of Canterbury penneknyff and his bootes, and divers skulls for the hedache; peces of the holie crosse able to make a whole crosse of; other reliques for rayne and certain other superstitiouse usages, for avoyding of wedes growing in corne, with suche other." All the relics mentioned can be identified; the skull for the headache was that of St Petronilla; the relic for rain and to prevent tares growing in corn was the arm of St Botolph. Moreover, apart from St Edmund himself, about whom the Commissioners are absolutely silent, there were no other major relics in the Abbey. Even more curious, there is a piece of deception in the list: "the pieces of the Holy Cross able to make a whole Cross of" was the copy of the Volto Santo at Lucca which had been given to Abbot Leofstan in the middle of the eleventh century and which hung in the chapel of the Cross. The real relic of the Cross was a tiny fragment lying on the breast of St Edmund. However, it appeared in the inventories and consequently had to be accounted for. Hence the deception. One important minor relic was missing from the list: St Edmund's cup. It is very doubtful if it would have been lumped together with the church plate. It looks at though Abbot Reeve managed to rescue it and the legends of its survival seem based on fact.

The second letter was written a few days later but is undated. It contains the sentence so famous for its ambiguity: "Pleasith it your lordship to be advertysed that wee have ben at saynt Edmondes Bury, where we founde a riche shryne whiche was very comberous to deface."
Of one of the most famous relics in England, not a word!

What possible explanations can there be? The most obvious is that Abbot Reeve had hidden it. This seems to have been fairly generally believed. There is scarcely a manor house or hall, once the property of the Abbey, which has not its legend that St Edmund's remains are hidden there. In spite of its wellnigh impossibility, it is the sort of explanation which might have to be adopted were it not known that the relics were in Toulouse.

The second explanation, that of Sir Ernest Clarke, has already been mentioned: the relics were pulverized in the fire of 1465. This also seems to have had its adepts at the time. "Less than a hundred years after the destruction of the shrine", writes Sir Ernest "William

Hawkins a schoolmaster of Hadleigh, whilst on a visit to Bury, made a particular search for the resting place of St Edmund's bones. He says in his latin poem "Corolla Varia" published in Cambridge in 1634 that the bones of St Edmund were nowhere to be found, and that the very site scarcely remained. 'The fire has devoured, and the winds which sweep everything, have scattered the ashes'. " Master Hawkins' latin is prettier than Sir Ernest's English:: "Flamma momordit, difflarunt cinerem, qui verrunt omnia venti." Suffolk schoolmasters are not a race to be despised. However, the pulverization theory simply cannot hold water.

Dr Montague James' explanation is much more interesting. When writing his admirable History of the Abbey published in 1895 he supposed that the shrine was merely defaced and the relics left unmolested, to be given decent burial at a later date. As late as 1944 A. F. Webling adopted the same theory in his historical novel "The Last Abbot". In view of the known instructions to the Commissioners, however, James had abandoned this opinion by 1901. He then argued that the relics must have been destroyed in 1539 because, had the Commissioners not found them, they would have blazed the fact abroad, delighted to have so gratuitous a proof of the fraudulence of monks as to find empty a shrine which reputedly contained an incorrupt body. Surely this argument is so convincing as to require special attention.

Some reconstruction is necessary. The Commissioners, like everybody else except the major officers of the Abbey, presumed that the incorrupt body of St Edmund was in the shrine. The destruction of so venerable an object would not be carried out secretly. The presence would be required of the whole community of monks, not only for their edification but also to give receipts for any valuable ornaments found with the body, such as the relief a foot long of St Michael in solid gold which was known to decorate the inner coffin. However "comberous" they may have found the bottom part to deface, they can have had no difficulty with the reliquary itself. The jewels, ornaments and silver plating having been carefully removed, the wooden hood could be prised open in a trice. What did the Commissioners find beneath it? There are three possible alternatives.

Firstly, what they expected: the incorrupt body of the Martyr. This they would have desecrated with unfeigned delight and reported the matter to Cromwell in the minutest detail.

Secondly, what Sir Ernest Clarke expected: some ashes and a few charred bones, the remains of the fire of 1465. It is under these circumstances, surely, that the Commissioners would have trumpeted the fraudulence of the monks: their incorrupt body turns out to be no more than a handful of dust.

But thirdly, supposing they found nothing at all? There would be a moment of agonizing silence. No matter what Abbot Reeve might say, no matter if he had warned them that the shrine was empty, the Commissioners would believe that he had stolen the body and hidden it elsewhere.

Their position would be unenviable. If they admitted to Cromwell that they had found no body then either they would stand self-accused of being cheated by a set of monks, or, far worse, Cromwell would accuse them of accepting bribes from the Abbot. This latter alternative would be the more disastrous in that they almost certainly did. Not only is there the matter of St Edmund's cup, but the Abbot's pension was considerably larger than might have been expected: he had the means to bribe. True, he only lived to enjoy it until March 31st, 1540, but that could not of necessity have been foreseen on November 5th, 1539, although Reeve should have remembered that Edmund was "a terrible protector of my own". On the other hand, if the Commissioners pretended that they had destroyed the body, what would happen if the Abbot produced it at a later date? They believed the body to be easily identifiable because they supposed it incorrupt.

No, Montague James' hypothesis appears more plausible than it really is. The only acceptable explanation for the Commissioners' silence on the subject of one of the most famous relics in the realm is that they never found it.

Perhaps it is idle to labour the point but it is more than a little suggestive that a body so often verified between 869 and 1198 should never again have been seen in Bury in spite of a new shrine, a vast conflagration and the destruction of the Abbey. It also implies an unusual prescience on the part of the Canons of St Sernin to have been claiming possession of relics which were in fact to be found absent from their proper shrine at the time of an unforeseen Reformation.

Bury Free Press Photograph

(xix) Great Gate.

Bury Free Press Photograph

(xx) St James' Gate Tower.

Bury Free Press Photograph

(xxi) Remains of West front of Abbey.

Bury Free Press

(xxii) Choir Altar site.

Bury Free Press

(xxiii) West wall of Crypt looking up at Choir Altar site.
Over Crypt was High Altar behind which rested the relics and Shrine of St Edmund.

Bury Free Press Photograph

(xxiv) Crypt viewed from Chapel of St Botolph looking towards
Lady Chapel under which were traces of an earlier Church of St Edmund

(xxv) North Transept viewed from The Treasury.

Bury Free Press

Bury Free Press Photograph

(xxvi) The Abbot's Bridge showing procession way in front.

(xxvi) Exterior of the Abbot's Bridge.

Bury Free Press Photograph

CHAPTER TEN

Toulouse until the Revolution

Since no bones have been produced in Bury, one had better return to Toulouse, where in the lower crypt were the bones of St Gilbert of Sempringham and of Saint Aymund, alias Eadmundus.

The Canons duly recited his office and celebrated his mass on November 20th of each year. There was sufficient public veneration for him to remain a patron of the town and his fresco to be restored in 1575. But he was becoming fairly shadowy, because he did not form part of the pilgrimage; no relic of his was in the deambulatory cupboards. Then on December 1st, 1581, Edmund Campion was killed at Tyburn.

Naturally enough, the average, agnostic Englishman, unless he has travelled the Continent and is interested in art, has no idea of the impact caused by the English Catholic Martyrs of the Reformation. He will not have seen San Stefano Rotondo in Rome, Sant' Elmo in Naples, the Zurburans from the Charterhouse of Seville, to name but three of the major works of art commemorating the English martyrs. Of these martyrs, apart from Saints Thomas More and John Fisher, the one to receive the most publicity was certainly Edmund Campion. This was not only due to his pre-eminence but also because he was a Jesuit and the Jesuits were everywhere, including Toulouse. It is only natural that members of the Society of Jesus should have propogated devotion to one of their own brethren martyred for the Faith.

As though Campion had not been enough to revive interest in the name of Edmund, a second Jesuit called Edmund was martyred on August 28th, 1628, Father Edmund Arrowsmith. Arrowsmith may have been a lesser man than Campion, but the "Relatio" of his death by an eye-witness, printed in 1630, is a singularly moving document. It certainly found its way to the Jesuit's library at Toulouse.

Precisely at this time, early in 1628, the Plague ravaged Toulouse. It went on and on, right through 1629 and 1630. By the summer of 1631 the situation was desperate. "All trade was brought to a halt. Grass was growing in the deserted streets as in the fields. There was scarcely a house which was neither abandoned nor contaminated. . . . . It was heart-rending to see wretched children, who had lost both father and mother and all means of support, more surely exposed to starvation than to disease, ... " (Montchal quoted by Bordier p. 77). The Plague, in fact.

Desperate plights suggest desperate remedies. Here were these English Edmunds dying for the honour of God while the original Edmund, a patron of the City, lay neglected, almost forgotten in the lower crypt of St Sernin. On August 12th, 1631, the "Sieurs Capitouls" (Chief Magistrates of Toulouse) vowed publicly and in due legal form to repair their neglect of St Edmund by giving him proper reliquaries and prayed to God to end the scourge at his intercession. Forthwith the plague ceased.

Of course after such devastation it took some years for Toulouse to get back to normal. The vow of 1631 was only put into effect in 1644. On July 16th of that year Archbishop Charles de Montchal, with a host of dignataries and notaries, opened the stone sarcophagus bearing the inscription "in big black lettering": "here lies the venerable body of St Edmund, Martyr, King of England". He proceeded to a canonical verification of the relics with the usual catalogue of the remains. The skull was complete. The lower jaw was detached and contained seven teeth in place. There were three loose teeth from the upper jaw. The skeleton was complete except for one radial; the other radial was partly missing as was a portion of one cubital. From these details the skull and skeleton remain to this day easily identifiable.

In this catalogue of remains, there are rather fewer teeth than might have been expected, but perhaps St Edmund was not quite as young as the Bury Life made him out to be. Besides, at his martyrdom, he was beaten with cudgels and some of his teeth may have been knocked out. But what has happened to the missing radial? The most probable explanation is that to preserve the rest, Ailwin had to surrender a part to Bishop Alphun in 1013. Abbot Samson seems to have been particularly interested in one of the arms when he examined the body in 1098. Was he looking to see how the radial had been extracted?

Montchal placed the skull in one solid silver reliquary made by a smith called Bernard Bruchon. The skeleton was placed in another, of monumental size, also of solid silver, with columns supporting a dome, made by Defaure and Loret. After the splendid ceremonies on St Edmund's Day the skeleton was placed above a new St Edmund's altar in the lower crypt and the skull was put into one of the cupboards of the deambulatory. There they remained, receiving the grateful veneration of the people, until the Revolution, when the two sets of relics have a slightly different history.

Toulouse appears to have lagged behind the rest of France in its revolutionary activities. The Civil Constitution of the Clergy was decreed in July 1790 but the non-juror curé-chanoine Castillon was left unmolested at St Sernin until May, 1791. He was then ousted and replaced by the juror, Père Hubert, ex-provincial of the Minims. As is well known, throughout the Revolution the Vicars General managed to keep some sort of contact with the juring priests, in spite of their being excommunicated for accepting the Civil Constitution. Throughout the revolutionary period the Vicar General of Toulouse was a certain Mgr du Bourg. What happened to the relics at that time is taken from a deposition he made in June, 1807, to his successor, Mgr Clément de Barbazan.

The Commissaires de la République arrived at St Sernin on February 27th, 1794. They stripped the place of all metal: altar-frontals, reredoses, tabernacles, candlesticks—everything went. The reliquaries went too. The relics, however, were removed in the presence of Père Hubert and of the guardian of the relics, one Sieur Aubert. The latter removed the relics from each reliquary, wrapped them in strips of cotton and replaced them in their proper positions. The whole process was witnessed by Père Hubert, who himself locked the cupboards in which the relics had been replaced.

The Civil Constitution of the Clergy was abolished on September 18th, 1794. Here again, Toulouse seems to have been late in the uptake. According to Mgr du Bourg, it was only in March, 1795, that Père Hubert was dismissed and Saint Sernin was closed. It was then rumoured that the Basilica was going to be razed to the ground. A Père Cassé, a Franciscan Observantine, decided to save the relics. He obtained a key to a side door from one Antoine Passerieux, Assistant Sacristan in the bad old days. On March 22nd, along with three laymen, Messieurs Limes, Pontier and Labat, he entered Saint Sernin. They took what they could in the time out of the cupboards of the deambulatory down to the upper crypt, where they made packages of the relics, sealed and numbered them and carried them off to the house of Pontier, who ran a boarding school. They returned on the 23rd to collect some more. They found that the only door to which they had a key had in the meantime been bolted from the inside.

In July, those relics removed from St Sernin were taken to the private house of the Comtesse de Comminges, where they were placed in proper boxes, numbered and sealed again. By this time the religious persecution was over. On July 23rd, the relics were returned in procession to St Sernin. The Vicar General, Mgr du Bourg, himself led the way, while the children of Pontier's school carried the relics. It must have been a moving sight: the old priest, the handful of faithful and the children with their boxes of bones. It was then established on the evidence of the laymen present on March 22nd as on July 23rd that the relics which they had not had time to remove had remained in the same position in which they had been left.

Again Toulouse lags behind. Everywhere else in France, churches were restored to public worship in October, 1796. Not so St Sernin. Although the Vicar General had access to it as early as July, 1795, the building was in fact returned to the ecclesiastical authorities only on November 14th, 1802. The first inventory of relics is dated 1804, without day or month. It reads: "In the chapel known as St Julitta's, the body of St Edmund King of England, in a wooden reliquary, double-boxed (i.e. one box inside another), the inner one locked with a padlock to which the key is broken"; then, in the chapel of St Hilarius, "coffer No. 5 with a strip of white paper sealed at each end with the text—relic of St Eadmont, King of England". As is perfectly clear from the more detailed inventory of 1807, Coffer No. 5. contained the skull; the box with the padlock whose key was broken contained the skeleton.

The two lots had had a slightly different history during the Revolution. The skull had been taken by Père Cassé and had received the seals and inscription from Mme de Comminges. The skeleton had been packed in an old box for removal on March 23rd, but in fact stayed where it was. The two parts thus recovered were given a new bronze reliquary by Archbishop d'Astros in 1845, as were the remains of St Gilbert of Sempringham.

The treatment of the relics during and after the revolution has been dealt with in some detail because it has considerable bearing on the principal argument against their authenticity which was produced by Sir Ernest Clarke during the polemics of 1901.

Beyond a doubt this was the thunderbolt which struck Cardinal Vaughan. Sir Ernest considered the argument unanswerable. He first describes the deplorable state of St Sernin during the Revolution, which is fair enough. He then raises his tone. The passage is too long to quote in full but the following will suffice: "The description given by M. d'Aldeguier (President of the Soc. Arch. du Midi, vol. for 1854) of what was done in St Edmund's chapel at Toulouse in 1853 is so interesting that I translate it in extenso. ' ... In a remote part of the crypt was found a stone tomb bearing the inscription Tomb of St Edmund. It contained a wooden chest in three compartments, in which were enclosed without particular designation a great number of bones. They were wrapped with care in silken stuffs and put back in the same chest. . . . and the Abbé Crepel performed on the same day a religious ceremony in honour of the unknown relics (reliques inconnues).' With such a pedigree as this reasonable men will, I think, hardly be disposed to accept the bones which were landed at Newhaven on the 25th of last month as the veritable skeleton of the great East Anglian King, Martyr and Virgin . . . . "

It seems unanswerable. Unfortunately, like Sir Ernest's "Confessor of a King of England", it happens to be rubbish. The stone sarcophagus found in the crypt in 1853 was that in which St Edmund had lain until 1644, when he was translated to the famous Montchal reliquaries. It still appears to have borne the inscription in big black lettering. But in 1853, St Edmund had been out of it for 209 years! He was at that time in Archbishop d'Astros' reliquaries, made as recently as 1845. As for the relics in the sarcophagus being unknown, a careful comparison with the list of 1807 will show that they belonged to the roman martyrs, Saints Symphorian, Claudius, Nicostrates, Castor and Simplicius.

CHAPTER ELEVEN

Arundel

The polemics of 1901 have been mentioned from time to time. The situation was not without its humour. Cardinal Vaughan was busy building Westminster Cathedral. It was customary in those days to have the relics of a martyr in all Catholic altars. What martyr should the Cardinal place in the high altar of his cathedral? Obviously St Edmund, once patron of England and now available at Toulouse, was the best choice. He wrote to Archbishop Germain asking him for the relics. To his immense surprise Germain refused to surrender one of the patrons of his city. Disappointed, Vaughan appealed over the Archbishop's head to the Pope. Eventually Archbishop Germain consented to surrender the skeleton, but not the skull, to Leo XIII, who in turn handed it over to Cardinal Vaughan. Thus the body of St Edmund travelled all the way from Toulouse to Rome and from Rome to England. In fact, by dint of some rather discreditable bullying, Vaughan got his way.

The body arrived at Newhaven on July 25th, 1901, accompanied by Archbishop, later Cardinal, Merry del Val, and was deposited, pending the completion of Westminster Cathedral, in the FitzAlan Chapel in Arundel parish church. There it remained over the nights of July 25th and 26th, lit by golden lamps lent by the Duke of Norfolk and watched by holy nuns. At 8.30 a.m. on Friday 26th, the relics were moved to the Duke's private Chapel in Arundel Castle. The Catholic schoolchildren led the way, followed by acolytes with lighted candles, then four priests carrying the relics, escorted by six others with lighted tapers. There followed Cardinal Vaughan, the Duke of Norfolk, the Lady May Howard, Archbishops Merry del Val and Stonor, and four lesser Bishops; lastly the throng. In fact it was all done in proper, Vaughan style. After a short panegyric from the Cardinal during Mass, the relics were deposited in an alcove in the south wall of the Chapel where they still remain.

So far so good. Unfortunately, on August 2nd, Dr Montague James of Trinity, Cambridge, wrote a letter to the Times denying the authenticity of the relics; his main thesis has already been dealt with. Not to be outdone, Dr Charles Bigg of Christ Church, Oxford, wrote in the same vein on August 13th. Then came the shattering blow from Sir Ernest Clarke on September 5th, which has already received more than its due in the preceding pages.

In front of such a barrage of experts, what was the poor Cardinal to do? There really appeared to be a dilemma: either the monks of Bury had been encouraging devotion for some 300 years at an empty shrine, or the Cardinal Archbishop of Westminster was about to encourage devotion to false relics. In either case Roman Catholics would be shown up as the deceivers which, in 1901, every Englishman knew them to be! It is hoped, however, that the present study has shown that the question was not quite as simple as that.

Anyway, without consulting Toulouse, without seeking the advice of a historian but only of a clairvoyant, on a sudden impulse, at a public meeting held in the Albert Hall on September 9th, Cardinal Vaughan caved in. He admitted to having been convinced by the arguments of Sir Ernest Clarke: the "Confessor of a King of England", the "Unknown Relics of 1853", the "pulverised bones of 1465" and all! He promised, of course, to set up an historical commission to examine the affair. He never did.

It really is rather comic: the unscrupulous bullying of Archbishop Germain and the craven submission to Sir Ernest Clarke; the tapers and procession of July 26th; and the abysmal surrender of September 9th. It makes one despair of the sanity of bishops.

Naturally enough, Archbishop Germain of Toulouse was not best well pleased. Much against his will he had sent St Edmund's skeleton to Rome, whence it was forwarded to England, and the net result was that the authenticity of his skull was called in question. Unlike Vaughan he set up a competent commission to examine the problem of his skull's authenticity. This was easy enough in Toulouse, the seat of an ancient and respected University. The Commission consisted of six members; the parish priest of St Sernin, one Canon Lawyer, one theologian, and three professional historians, one of whom was rather eminent in his day, Jean Lestrade, Secretary General of the Archaeological Society of Southern France. They produced their Report in December, 1902. Archbishop Germain did not publish it as he was waiting for Cardinal Vaughan to do the like. It got lost and was eventually unearthed in 1964. The present study owes much to it. Perhaps it is sufficient here to quote its conclusion: "Le culte séculaire que les fidèles rendent aux reliques de St Edmond, roi d'Angleterre, Confesseur et Martyr, dans l'insigne Basilique de St Sernin, remplissant d'ailleurs les conditions requises par les saints

Canons pour être l'objet d'un culte publique, garde par là même son prestige et sa legitimité." Such "frenchery" defies translation. What it means is that the relics are all right.

Hence arose the amusing situation that the relics of St Edmund were authentic in France but not in England. Had the Arundel skeleton been shipped back to Toulouse, doubtless it would have become authentic in mid-Channel. Just how unauthentic the skeleton had become in England can be gleaned from Goodwin's "Abbey of Bury St Edmunds" (Blackwood, 1931). "On the sole authority of a seventeenth century book of devotion 'propre pour exciter la dévotion des fidèles qui la liront,' Pierre de Caseneuve's Vie de Saint Edmond (1644), it was formally believed in some quarters that the relics had been captured by Louis and given to the Church of St Sernin at Toulouse. This supposition was first shown to be incorrect by Sir Edward (sic) Clarke." In the 1950's it was even suggested that the Arundel relics could be got rid of by being buried in the churchyard.

St Edmund appears to have held other views concerning his remains. The story is given here as it appears in M. Bordier's book, Vivant St Edmond (Editions du Cèdre, 1961).

"St Edmund was far from my thoughts on that day in August, 1942, when I wandered into St Sernin at Toulouse. I had time to spare between two trains and the friend with whom I had been staying for a few days in the neighbourhood had said to me: If you like Romanesque architecture you ought to have a look at St Sernin."

At that time, M. Bordier was not a practising Catholic.

"I cannot recollect my feelings as I wandered down the nave. My memory becomes vivid precisely at that point when, strolling round the deambulatory I noticed a group of people waiting by a door; they were going to visit the crypt. As I have said I had time to spare: I joined the group. The guide herded us together on a landing in the upper crypt and started explaining things. I paid no attention, as, almost straight away, I left the group and went down one of the two staircases which led to the lower crypt—I took the one on the right.

"At the bottom, I was in semi-darkness and made my way very slowly round the crypt, towards the right. I was not looking at anything and I was thinking of nothing. I remember it as of yesterday; I was in a state of peaceful bliss, of void, of abandonment. Suddenly, at the corner at the far end, I stopped and stood to attention as if on a parade ground; for a few seconds perhaps. Then, rather like waking after a dream, I thought: what am I doing here? Why am I here? In front of me was a vaulted recess, not very deep but dark and closed off by an iron grille. Inside was a tomb, a sarcophagus, which appeared to me to be very old. It was covered with dust. I bowed my head and at my feet saw an inscription on the base of the sarcophagus. I found it difficult to decipher although it was in large capital letters but worn by the passage of years:

S. Eadmundus.

"Eadmundus, Edmond—no it couldn't be! The St Edmund of November 20th, from whom I had acquired my Christian name, was an English King: I had looked that up in a dictionary when I was a boy. This tomb at Toulouse could not be his ... yet at the same time I felt an interior conviction that I had been led to that spot, halted in front of that recess.

"The group was still in the upper crypt. I climbed the stairs and bought a guide book. In a few lines I learned that the body of St Edmund, martyred by the Danes on November 20th, 870, had been brought to France by Lewis VIII and left with the Canons of St Sernin at the time of the Albigensian Crusade."

So far the story is perfectly straightforward. M. Bordier had felt one of those moments of intense and vivid experience of reality, such as most people sometimes have in life. It happened to coincide with his unexpected discovery of the tomb of his patron saint. That is all. There was no sudden conviction, no miracle of conversion; just the vivid memory of an intense experience.

Conversion came, but gradually and painfully over the years. But when it came it was somehow associated with the experience at St Sernin. Ten years later M. Bordier decided to make a little pilgrimage to Toulouse on November 20th in thanksgiving for his conversion.

"I learned that there would be a mass of St Edmund, as there was each year, at eight o'clock in the crypt. When I returned a few women were waiting at the door. The keeper opened up and we followed him down the stairs, each carrying our chair. I could have found my way blindfolded to that corner at the far end where I had been led ten years previously, but when I got there instead of the dark recess, choked by the dust of centuries as I had seen it, instead of the sarcophagus which I could have touched through the grille, there was a well-lit chapel, rather ornate. At the back stood an altar and above it a bronze reliquary. The altar frontal was composed of painted panels and across them in gilt letters was written: "S. Eadmundus." ... The keeper was waiting for me to lock the crypt. "What has been going on down there?" I asked. "The tomb behind the grille with the inscription at my feet at the base of the sarcophagus. Everything has been changed?" He stared at me: "Nothing has been changed since the Chapel was restored a hundred years ago."

"What I had seen twenty years before I recognised immediately when, working on this book I came across the description of the tomb of St Edmund as it had been in 1644 ... The dust, the neglect of ages, was the state of my soul."

Whatever may be the spiritual significance of M. Bordier's experience, its historical importance lies in the fact that it induced him to write his book. It was intended to be a hagiography and a work of piety; almost by accident it happens to be very scholarly. For the first time there was a critical study of the Toulouse evidence. As has been seen, it turns out to be very much more substantial than Goodwin's "sole authority of a seventeenth century book of devotion", which has not even been mentioned in these pages.

A further result of Bordier's work was the revival of interest at Toulouse in St Edmund. This led to 1964 to the discovery in the archives of St Sernin of the complete dossier of Archbishop Germain's Commission of 1901-2. It had not been catalogued and was mis-filed. Indeed, it would be a great boon to students if the archives at St Sernin could be competently catalogued and a copy of the catalogue made available at the admirably kept Municipal Library. The archives of the Département of the Haute Garonne have been re-housed. The archivist's department could not be more helpful, but even here there are bundles of papers from St Sernin which are rather summarily catalogued. One would have thought that several B. Litts would have been obtainable at Toulouse University for introducing a little order into this chaos.

It was the discovery of the findings of Archbishop Germain's Commission which led me as the Roman Catholic Parish Priest at Bury St Edmunds, to attempt to obtain the return of the Arundel relics to Bury. Prior to the discovery, I believed the relics to be authentic on historical grounds, but, as far as Canon Law was concerned there was no ecclesiastical document to maintain their authenticity more recent than 1644, and this had been rejected by Cardinal Vaughan in 1901. Short of asking the Archbishop of Westminster to establish an historical Commission, which he would be most unlikely to do, there was nothing for it but to leave the Arundel relics un-recognised, unhonoured. The discovery of the Toulouse Commission altered the situation. In Canon Law, the Toulouse relics, and consequently the skeleton at Arundel, could licitly be objects of public veneration. After all, the findings of an Archbishop of Toulouse, after seeking advice from a competent commission, were worth rather more than the obiter dicta of an Archbishop of Westminster after seeking advice from a soothsayer. It was absurd that the skull should be venerated in Toulouse and the skeleton rejected at Arundel. If St Edmund could complain of neglect at Toulouse prior to 1644, it was as nothing in comparison to the neglect in England in 1964.

On December 23rd of that year, I started negotiations to bring the Arundel relics back to Bury. Permission to receive them was given by the Roman Catholic Bishop of Northampton. The Archbishop of Westminster waived his rights to them. The Bishop of Southwark, in whose Diocese Arundel then was, would not object to their removal. By February, 1965, it looked as though the translation would certainly take place.

It did not. All the arguments of 1901 against the authenticity of the relics were duly rehearsed. Anyway, the proper place for them was not St Edmund's Church but St James' Cathedral, where the construction of the fine new choir had just started. It seemed as though the authenticity of the relics would depend on where they went. The Lord Lieutenant was asked to intervene. The Duke of Norfolk was requested not to let the relics out of his possession. It was astonishing how much heat the bones of St Edmund, now cold for nearly eleven hundred years, could still generate! They stayed where they were. All that I got were the three loose teeth from St Edmund's upper jaw, which were sent to Bury from Toulouse by Archbishop Garonne in 1966.

Such is a brief summary of the story of St Edmund, alive and dead. Alive, he was a Christian King and an Englishman unwilling to compromise. His personal failure, his martyrdom, supplied the inspiration to English national unity. For over three centuries he was Patron of the land. Few corpses can have inspired the loving care which his incorrupt body inspired. On the other hand, the relics of few saints can have been so neglected.

Relics are unfashionable. Nevertheless it somehow seems improper that the mortal remains of a saintly king and patron of England should lie discredited in a private chapel. If the petty jealousies of men prevent their being brought to St Edmund's Church in St Edmund's

Borough, then perhaps they should be returned to Toulouse. There, in the company of St Gilbert of Sempringham, St Edmund might receive from strangers the honour denied him by his countrymen.

Index by Dates

775. Charlemagne's conquest of Saxony.

794. King Ethelbert of East Anglia murdered by Offa of Mercia.

841? (probably earlier) birth of Edmund in Saxony.

854. Arrival of Edmund in Norfolk.

855. Christmas Day, Coronation of Edmund at Bures.

865. First Danish invasion.

868. Siege of Nottingham with Alfred.

869. November 20th, Martyrdom of St Edmund.

878. Conversion of Guthrum, who becomes Athelstan II of East Anglia.

880? Canonization and Translation of St Edmund to Boedericsworth.

909. Probable date of Dunstan's birth.

926. Verification of the body by Bishop Theodred.

929. Visit of Athelstan of England with Dunstan to Boedericsworth.

960? Verification by the impious nobleman, Leofstan.

985. Abbo wrote Dunstan's account of the Passion of St Edmund.

990 or 992. The monk Ailwin appointed to guard the relics.

1010-1013. Ailwin carries the relics to London.

1021. Ailwin becomes Bishop. The Benedictines are brought from Hulme. Boedericsworth becomes St Edmund's Borough.

1032. Consecration of Cnut's Church with verification of the relics by Ailwin.

1050. Verification of the relics by Abbot Leofstan.

1071. Archdeacon Hermann's original History, now lost. The existing version, as amended at Bury St Edmunds, could be as late as 1090.

1095. Translation and Verification by Abbot Baldwin upon the building of the great Abbey Church.

1150. Geoffrey of Wells' account of St Edmund's childhood.

1198. Abbot Samson's verification. Jocelin of Brakelond.

1217. Theft of the relics by the Viscount of Melun.

1219. Lewis leaves the relics at St Sernin, Toulouse.

1272. Death of Jeanne of Toulouse and of Henry III of England. Likely date for the proclamation of St Edmund as Patron of Toulouse and for the news to reach Bury St Edmunds.

1275. Destruction of St Edmund's Chapel at Bury St Edmunds. No verification of the relics.

1284. The cross of St George appears on the seal of Lyme Regis.

1429-1446. Abbot Curteys. The Age of Aggregations.

1465. The great fire at Bury St Edmunds. No verification of the relics.

1470? First unofficial document at Toulouse claiming St Edmund.

1489, 1504, 1534. Official documents at Toulouse claiming St Edmund.

1515. Maitre Bertrand's "Gesta Tholosanorum".

1539. The Dissolution at Bury St Edmunds. No verification or mention of the incorrupt body of St Edmund.

1575. Repainting of fresco to S. Eadmundus at Toulouse.

1631. Vow of Toulouse to St Edmund.

1644. The Montchal Reliquaries.

1794/5. The Revolution at Toulouse.

1845. The d'Astros Reliquaries.

1901. The skeleton of St Edmund at Arundel Castle.

1965. Attempt to move the skeleton to Bury St Edmunds.

1969/70. The 1100th anniversary of the Martyrdom.

Index

F

G

BURY ST. ED

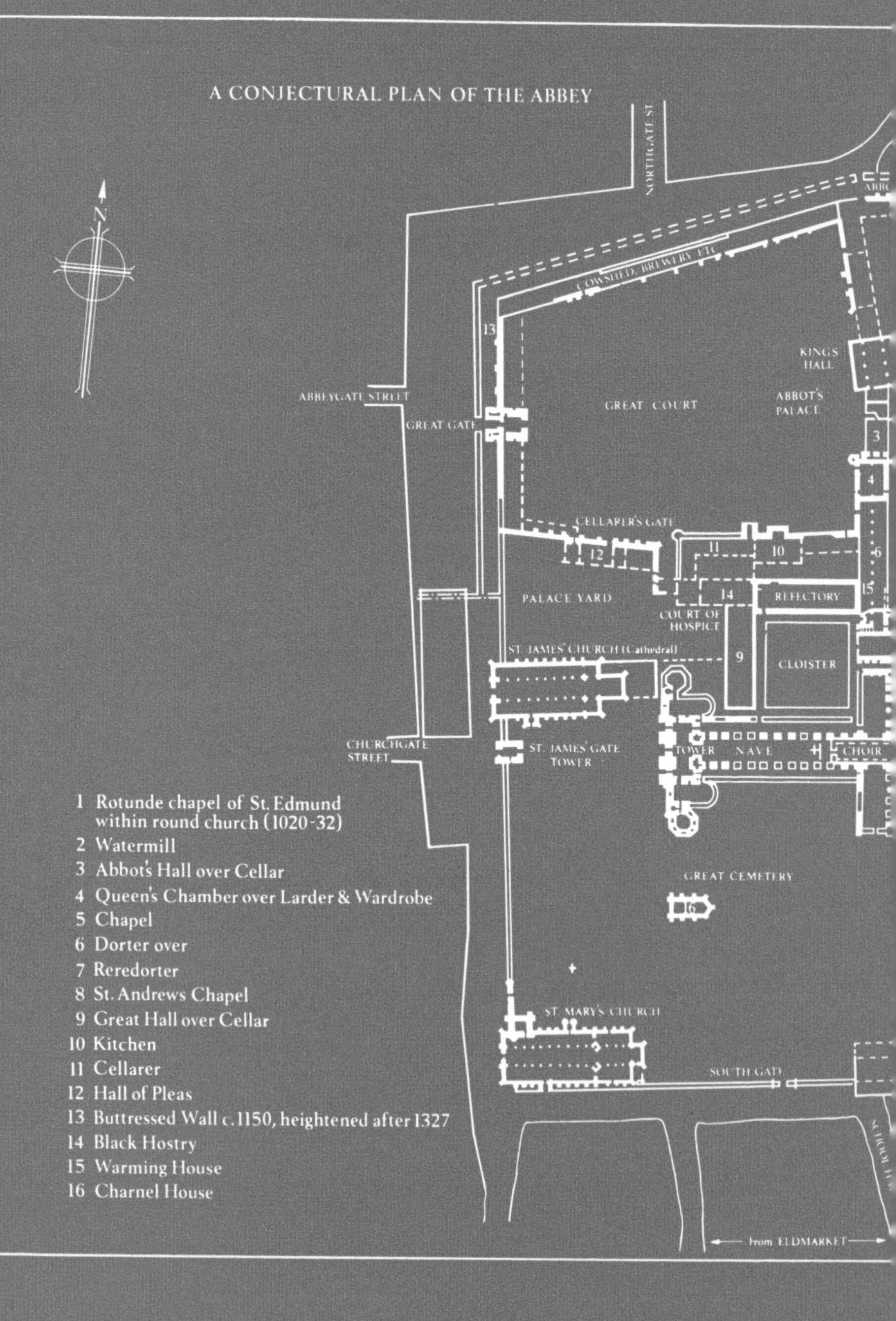
A CONJECTURAL PLAN OF THE ABBEY
N
NORTHGATE ST.
COWSHED, BREWERY ETC
KINGS HALL
ABBOT'S PALACE
GREAT COURT
ABBEYGATE STREET
GREAT GATE
CELLARER'S GATE
PALACE YARD
REFECTORY
COURT OF HOSPICE
ST. JAMES' CHURCH (Cathedral)
CLOISTER
CHURCHGATE STREET
ST. JAMES' GATE TOWER
TOWER
NAVE
CHOIR
GREAT CEMETERY
ST. MARY'S CHURCH
SOUTH GATE
from ELDMARKET
1 Rotunde chapel of St. Edmund within round church (1020-32)
2 Watermill
3 Abbot's Hall over Cellar
4 Queen's Chamber over Larder & Wardrobe
5 Chapel
6 Dorter over
7 Reredorter
8 St. Andrews Chapel
9 Great Hall over Cellar
10 Kitchen
11 Cellarer
12 Hall of Pleas
13 Buttressed Wall c. 1150, heightened after 1327
14 Black Hostry
15 Warming House
16 Charnel House